'Lucy and Hadrien are a tour-de-f
world. Lucy has taken PR and n
modern small businesses who v..... .. ..u.. u ...uu.
commercial impact with their campaigns. But it is only when
you layer in Hadrien's vivacious branding mind that you get
something truly revolutionary. The combination of their
mutually deep understanding of how to build a brand that not
only looks good but also speaks to its customers is unique
and incredibly effective. Having worked with them both
independently and together, I couldn't think of a better duo
to bring this book to life. The book, however, speaks for itself.'

**Albert Azis-Clauson,
CEO and co-founder, UnderPinned**

'The Wern is a wealth of inspiration and knowledge for small
businesses and brands from all walks of life. Lucy and Hadrien
truly understand what it takes to create an irresistible brand.
From the visual aspects, all the way to the core of what you
stand for as an individual, your brand is a kaleidoscope of
parts that work perfectly together. A must-have for every
entrepreneur out there.'

**Fab Giovanetti, marketing consultant, CEO and author
of *Reclaim your Time Off***

'As a former CMO I can tell you that in spite of the millions
spent on "branding" the majority of the industry consists of
expensive so-called "experts" whose aim is to take a relatively
simple thing and make it intimidating and complicated. In
Hype Yourself, Lucy took the PR industry and broke it down
in a simple, easy to understand manner that any founder
could apply to their business. Now with Hadrien alongside,
they've done the same with *Brand Yourself*, holding your
hand as you get your brand strategy sorted, show you how

to create a killer brand toolkit and how to spend smartly to make your brand famous. It's everything you need without the million dollar price tag attached.'

Jeff Taylor, founder and Editor in Chief, *Courier*

'I speak to so many people who have a vague understanding of branding. They know it's important and that it's "more than just a logo" but the terrifying process of working out who you are, what you stand for and how to convey your "everything" to the outside world, is a chore that most small businesses never fully complete. I think the main reason for this is because there has never been a real blueprint to follow, until now. Lucy and Hadrien have demystified the process of creating a strong identity. Follow the steps in this book and your brand will begin working for you while you sleep; by attracting the exact audience you wish to serve.'

David Speed, host of Creative Rebels podcast and artist

**LUCY WERNER &
HADRIEN CHÂTELET**

brand
yourself

A NO-NONSENSE
BRAND TOOLKIT FOR
SMALL BUSINESSES

First published in Great Britain by Practical Inspiration Publishing, 2021

ISBN   9781788602730   (print)
        9781788602754   (epub)
        9781788602747   (mobi)

Practical Inspiration
Publishing

CONTENTS

INTRODUCTION

QUOTE

IT ALL STARTS WITH A STORY.

Hadrien Châtelet

businesses with great brands to spark your own creative brand implementation ideas. This is the part of the book that will be chock-full of inspiration.

Chapter 5: The next branding leap. There are thousands of branding agencies and designers out there. How do you pick the right one or how do you even brief them?

As ever, the work has to be done by you… but hopefully you can see from this quick overview that we will be here with you the whole way. We'll be cheering you on, and giving lots of ideas and support – alongside you for every step. Now, buckle up… and let's get busy branding!

CHAPTER 1

HOW TO COMPILE YOUR BRAND STRATEGY

QUOTE

A BEAUTIFUL BRAND IS AMAZING, BUT A MEANINGFUL ONE IS BETTER.

Hadrien Châtelet

Before we get really stuck in to the hard work of building your brand strategy, let's take a look at exactly what we're talking about when we talk about branding.

WHAT IS BRANDING EXACTLY? WHAT ISN'T IT?

Branding is a dynamic process. It is more than just your product, logo or colour palette. It's about your reputation. It's what your audience feel about your product, service or company. But mainly, it's what they remember about you. In that way, PR and branding cross over. It's why Hadrien and I combine a lot of our strategic thinking across our clients. Done well, your brand, just like publicity, is about conveying a *feeling* to your audience.

Honestly, if I had a pound for every time a small business owner approached us and asked for a logo, thinking that was their brand, we'd be a very rich agency. It's a common misconception that creating your brand starts with a logo design, but a logo is just a symbol. It is something that helps your consumer to remember who is talking and what their behaviour is. This is why logos are often the avatars (or profile pics) for social media channels, because on seeing them we instantly understand who is communicating.

The brand is more than just your colours and fonts, too. These are all part of what creates the look and feel, but it's the whole package that conveys your emotion. Think of it like this: Hadrien wears colourful clothes, but that doesn't *define* his personality; it is simply another element that makes up the tapestry of who he is. If you were to take the clothes away, brand Hadrien still exists (albeit slightly chillier). It should be the same with your own brand.

Another misconception we often come across is that the brand is the product. Again, this is only one small part of the overall picture – branding isn't about something physical or tangible. Flyers, marketing materials and the way your product looks and feels can operate as part of the promotional tool of the brand, but they don't embody the emotion and feeling of the overarching brand.

As we can see from all of these misconceptions, there's a common thread: a lot of small businesses think that branding is about the visual appearance of their business. And absolutely, having a good-looking website and an identifiable colour palette is going to help you – but this isn't what branding actually is. These things come from decisions you make about how to use your brand – in other words, *your visual identity comes from your brand strategy.*

The brand strategy is the business plan for your brand. When you create your brand, you need to think about what you want your audience to feel.

Let's take the concept of a book. You start with a preface or an introduction. This first part, like where we introduced ourselves to you, is where we set the scene. We explain where you are, where and who we are and where we're going to go together. Creating the brand is just that. It is scene-setting for your business. It's the look and feel, the culture. But more than that, it is the feeling, the heart, the emotion of the people that your audience get to experience when they work with you or buy from you.

So, let's dive straight in to how to build your brand strategy.

BRAND STRATEGY

This is the most important part of your branding exercise. There are millions of ways you can execute your brand to appeal to all of the senses, and millions of ways that brands can give you different emotions or connections with their audience. But there are only a few ways that are going to be successful for you. That is what we are trying to find – the exact set of conditions where your brand speaks in the right way, saying the right things, to the right audience.

One of the most important things for you to do, to help you find this set of conditions, is to define where you are going. You don't want to start this journey without a destination in mind – so a huge part of all the brand strategy steps that are in this chapter is about defining the goal that you are aiming for with your brand. This chapter is all about finding out where you are going, and planning how to get there.

To help us achieve this, we are going to run through the following sections:

- competitor research
- values
- vision
- mission
- purpose
- audience mapping
- brand behaviour.

Ready to get going? Great! Then grab your notebook, or download our branding playbook at hypeyourself.com/playbook.

COMPETITOR RESEARCH

Looking around you is the first place to start. While larger companies might have access to more expensive tools and resources to conduct competitor research for them, we want to show you that it doesn't have to be an expensive, time-consuming or overcomplicated process.

Look at your sector, your competitors, what is new, what is old – and learn from them. You can learn best practices as well as mistakes you need to avoid – so look for the good and the bad. There are probably a few companies that do the same services or are at least close to you and your product or service offering; look at how they are doing. They're potentially doing not too shabbily; if so, you can learn from what they are doing well and think about how you may wish to incorporate this behaviour. You may also have an idea of what they are doing badly – things you fundamentally do not want to be doing.

Like the old aphorism about keeping your friends close but your enemies closer, you need to really understand and know your competitors because otherwise you are going to struggle to define and market what it is about yourself that is unique. So checking your market and your competitive set is the first and most important step for all the prep work we will do in Chapter 1.

3. *You can be aware that what makes a consumer choose one brand over another is affinity and loyalty.* In many cases, a consumer will make a choice based on values that feel right for them. This can be an even stronger driver than price point.

Think about it in another way. If I were to ask you about friendships, you would probably tell me that you like a certain person because they are funny, elegant, intelligent… and so on. We all define why we want to be friends with a particular person over someone else. It's the same for your brand – defining your values is the exercise of understanding your proposition, your business or yourself in adjectives.

In the next activity we are going to start by expanding your values far and wide, and then help you drill down to just a few. This is important, because if you have more than three to five it becomes difficult to not be distracted or muddled about what you stand for.

1. *Who are you?* Start with a blank sheet in your playbook. Or maybe you could do this as a team with a whiteboard. Write down every adjective that is used to describe you. Include all of them, good and bad – this is not the time for barriers or judgement. If you get stuck, have a look at the words used on the next page.

VALUES

SUSTAINABLE   CARING
DEPENDABLE
INNOVATIVE   PASSIONATE
RESPECTFUL EXPERT
COMMITTED
BEAUTIFUL   COURAGEOUS
INSPIRING   QUALITY UNIQUE
FUN
DIVERSE   HONEST FRESH
RULE BREAKING   PLAYFUL LOUD
TIMELESS   MESMORIZING
CALM   IMPACTFUL   FAIR
SAFE   RELIABLE
ENTERTAINING   INTUITIVE
TALENTED   CORPORATE
ENERGETIC   LOYAL   MINDFUL
APPROACHABLE   CURIOUS
PROFESSIONAL
DRIVEN   DETERMINED   CREATIVE

After you have exhausted as many words as possible and everyone has contributed, have a look through the list and circle or mark up any words that resonate with you. Select a minimum of three and a maximum of five that define who you are.

2. *Who do others say you are?* For the next step, it's the same principle, only this time ask the people around you. This doesn't need to be mass testing – ask the people who know you and your business.

Ask them to select four or five words that describe you and your business. Start testing with your circle of friends and colleagues – what do people think about you? Larger businesses might do this by paying an external company, but you can start this with just your social circle. Ask people what they really think about you and hopefully they will not only help you identify your characteristics, but they might be able to put their finger on what is truly different and your key point of differentiation from someone else.

HACK

A really great tool to help you do this quickly is www.mentimeter.com – using the Word Cloud template. You can ask a question like: What adjective would you use to describe [insert your business name here]? –and enable the multiple-answer options. You will then start to get a really clear visual picture of the adjectives people most associate with you.

3. *What makes you different?* Write down everything positive that makes your brand different – don't worry about the order for now.

4. *What do you want people to remember about you?* It's one thing to know who you are, but it's another to know what you want people to think about you. Go back to your playbook list of words and now think about it in terms of how you want to be remembered. What mark do you want you or your business to leave on the world?

5. *Narrow it down.* Next, divide your list into categories. Notice if you have similar adjectives and group them together (e.g. if you are empowering people, and you have a whole bunch of words that relate to this, you can group them together under 'empowering').

6. *Sharpen.* Once you have done this, pick your top three to five values from across the board – these are your business's values.

EXAMPLE

VALUES

We recently developed a brand for Vevolution, who have built a platform for plant-based and cell-based businesses and investors to connect and grow. When it came to creating their new brand identity, we had the task of developing a new look and feel that encapsulated their freshly pivoted company.

Vevolution's mission is to accelerate the plant-based and cell-based business economy. They do this by providing technology solutions that connect start-ups, investors and the community. The Vevolution team are spread across Europe and America and adopt a modern and vibrant approach to business, placing innovation and technology at the heart of the business.

Here are the company's values:

**LOUD
MODERN
INSPIRING
ICONIC
OPEN**

We started with the adjective 'loud' because of the gravitas of the work and the impact it has, as well as acknowledging the company's eagerness to impart the feeling that this is more than just a technology platform. It's a movement.

'Modern', due to the market positioning. They are targeting and working with start-up and innovative companies.

The third adjective is 'inspiring' – when you listen to their journey and what they are trying to do, not just on the Vevolution platform but in the way they live, they change our perception; they are helping the world to be a better place, and this is amazingly inspiring. We wanted something that is empowering people and riding behind this idea of joining the movement to change the world.

And this is where we came across our fourth adjective, 'iconic', because we wanted the audience to be part of something that was iconic and timeless.

Finally, it was important to bring in the idea of being 'open' and accessible. Vegan or not, we would be welcomed by them and invited to become part of the journey and part of the movement.

Values are all about truly understanding what makes you special, and the elements and characters of the business that make up who you are.

Tips

- Don't worry about including everything on your list. It's great you have these additional words: these can be banked and used in marketing copy later! For the values, though, you really want to narrow them down to a maximum of three to five.
- If you find this exercise hard, don't worry – that's normal! Talking about and describing your top qualities can be an excruciating task. Persevere!
- Don't feel you have to pick from our list of words – this is only a suggestion if you get stuck. If you think of your own words, so much the better!
- Don't try to write an essay. This isn't a dissertation on who you are and where you come from. It's just about selecting simple adjectives.
- If you only have one point of view, there's a chance you could be thinking of yourself lower or higher than others would see you – asking others gives a fresh perspective.

- You may have a huge list but struggle to identify what the most important point is, so by asking others it will help to give you clarity on your values and ways to describe them.

VISION

This is another way of saying where you want to be in the future. What is the *vision* of your business? What do you dream about when you think about the future of the business? As we have said, when you start a journey you first must define where you would like to go. For example, a one-person home-organizing business might have a vision of turning the business into a franchise across the country or even internationally, with great customer satisfaction and perfect service.

Vision is what you want to do in your dreams.

So, your brand vision is like the crystal ball of your business dreams, and our job now is to turn that into a functioning paragraph. Having a clear vision is important for two reasons. First, it will make you *move* – a vision will force you to not be static, both you as a leader and your employees. Second, your vision should represent your 'eureka' moment, your 'I got it!' moment – it's your *big idea*, the one you are willing to sacrifice the next couple of years of your life to make succeed. When it gets tough or you feel lost, your vision will be your best friend, your strongest motivation and your northern light.

VISION

Using your playbook, look at the space for writing your vision. Write one or two sentences (or a paragraph maximum) that highlight what you are trying to achieve.

- Identify precisely the product or service you want to focus on.
- What scale do you want your business to be?
- Where would you like your business to have its office?
- Who does your business serve? Who are the customers, who are the staff?
- What special or unique way do you want your business to appear?

EXAMPLE

VISION

Here's an example from one of The Wern's clients, English 4 French, an English-language school in France. Their vision is: 'To revolutionise the way English is taught to French adults.' As you can see, it's just a one-liner. It's quite short, but it perfectly embodies what they are trying to do as a business.

Tips

- Try to be more specific than simply saying, 'I want to sell X'. Make it more defined, e.g. 'I want to sell X in the online world'.
- Keep it short, sweet and precise.
- Don't worry about the how and why of what you are doing, just dream of the big goal for the next five years.

MISSION

We have just defined your vision, or your destination. If the vision is your future, then defining your mission is the present; this is where we look at how you will get there. What daily action/routine will you do to achieve your goal? This might sound pretty neutral, but I promise that this stage will say a lot about you.

Think about it: let's say your vision is to reach Cairo, Egypt from London, UK, and you choose to go by bicycle and avoid staying in hotels – your mission becomes to go on a long-distance cycling adventure to Cairo. This tells me a lot about the type of person you are and the type of journey you are about to go on. It sends a clear and strong message to anyone watching too – all the cyclists and all the fans of adventures will watch you, follow you and support you on this journey because your mission appeals to them – it's a very different story than catching a luxury plane to Cairo.

So, setting your mission is defining the way you will go about doing your business at the present time.

MISSION

It's now time to write your mission statement using your playbook. Answer the following questions:

- What is your core offering? What are you doing on a daily basis?
- Who is your primary audience, your typical client?
- After they have experienced your product or services, what benefits will your client enjoy?
- What are the unique qualities or ways of doing things that you are offering to your client?

Using all the above answers, you now can put them together to form a short, unique and impactful mission statement.

MISSION

Mark Leruste is the founder of Ministry of Purpose and an award-winning podcast host and TEDx speaker. His mission statement is:

Through our talks, workshops and coaching programmes, we empower **entrepreneurs and business leaders** *to show up as their authentic selves, stand up for what they believe and become the spotlight in their industry.*

italics = present action defining what you do
bold = to whom
<u>underline</u> = the benefit

Tips

- Be as precise as you can be.
- Take the time to find something with gravitas.
- You might have difficulty finding something unique or with as much impact as the example above, and that's ok, but do try and make this specific to *you* so that you stand out from your competition.
- Make it as original, fundamental and memorable as possible.

PURPOSE

As we have discovered, branding is about your reputation. But why does your reputation matter so much?

Beauty and accessibility do not make you fall in love. All beauty and accessibility can lead to are short and meaningless relationships – when we fall in love, we fall in love with more than the nearest attractive thing. We fall in love with someone's small defects, our common interests, our common loves and hates and perhaps most crucially – with what we stand for. This is what creates true connection and long-lasting relationships – in business, as well as in romance.

To build a strong brand, the purpose should be the beating heart. It isn't just so you can make a difference and stand out – although of course, that is important. For a small business to be commercially successful and build a lasting brand, it is imperative to have purpose engrained and underpinning your service in an authentic way.

When we work to a bigger purpose:

1. We are more motivated with our mission and in turn this leads to better revenues.
2. When we explain our purpose it helps our audience to connect with us.
3. If you are building your own small business and reading this book, the chances are you want to try and leave the world a better place than how you found it. A purpose helps with that.

Having purpose at the heart of your business is *good business.*

The year 2020 taught us that purpose-driven business is here to stay. But don't panic; purpose provides clarity for your business and it makes you focus. This is a tool to help you improve your business and your brand – not something that you will necessarily be judged on! It doesn't need to be the leading message of your PR and marketing, so don't be afraid to dig deep. This can be for your eyes only.

Now you have a choice – the following activities are two of our favourite approaches that we find helpful in defining purpose. We have included both as separate activities for you to try – pick the one that seems to fit you best, or try both and see what you end up with!

PURPOSE

Let's start with the seven levels of 'why'[1]. If you can't find seven reasons then try to do at least three or four. Try to really dig deep inside of yourself with this thinking. You might start with the following:

1. You created product X because there was a gap in the market.
2. But *why* did you care about that gap in the market? Perhaps it is because it is a passion project of yours.
3. But *why* is it a passion project? Perhaps because it is something that you have been really good at.
4. But *why* are you good at it? Perhaps because as a child in your household growing up, this area was lacking so you made up for it by focusing on this space.
5. But *why* was it lacking? Perhaps you are a creative and you grew up in a strict professional household.
6. But *why* is it needed? Perhaps to bring fun and creativity to spark joy every day.

Go to your playbook and fill out the 'but why' section and keep digging at a deeper level. Once you have finished doing this a few times, have a good look through your answers.

How does it make you feel and reflect on your business?

How does it inform what you are doing for your business?

---

[1] This activity is used with permission from David Hieatt and the Do Lectures workshop. See https://thedolectures.com, originally influenced by Simon Sinek, *Start With Why* (2009).

PURPOSE

For some businesses the bigger purpose is baked into the foundations of the business. For others, it may be the first time you are considering this and it can be a confusing place to start. Entrepreneur and business expert Daniel Priestly introduced me to the United Nations (UN) global goals,[2] which are a great platform and an opportunity to align your business with a bigger universal purpose. The 17 UN global goals are:

1. No poverty.
2. Zero hunger.
3. Good health and well-being.
4. Quality education.
5. Gender equality.
6. Clean water and sanitation.
7. Affordable and clean energy.
8. Decent work and economic growth.
9. Industry, innovation and infrastructure.
10. Reduced inequality.
11. Sustainable cities and communities.
12. Responsible consumption and production.
13. Climate action.
14. Life below water.
15. Life on land.
16. Peace and justice strong institutions.
17. Partnerships to achieve the goals.

---

[2] See www.globalgoals.org.

Select one or two that resonate with you. It could be that you pick one with your head and one that connects with your heart.

HACK

Download the free UN global goals asset media pack and share across your business how you will be incorporating it into your daily work – not only to keep you accountable but so you can share your purpose with your audience.

EXAMPLE

PURPOSE

Tony's Chocolonely is a traditional chocolate factory with a twist – its purpose is to make 100% slave-free chocolate. It is not to produce the best chocolate or to give the best experience/services – all the other chocolate factories can fight over that! By defining its purpose, Tony's Chocolonely has created a brand-new market where it is king, a market where all the chocolate lovers and people who want to support this purpose (and that is a lot of potential consumers!) will be. This is an example of a purpose that has been made public-facing; yours does not need to be, but it will inform and relate to your mission and vision, which should be public-facing.

Tips

- Most people worry that the purpose is public-facing, but it is primarily for internal purposes, for you. It is for you to remember yourself, what you are doing it for and how you are going to get there.
- Be honest and really take the time to find your purpose. It's not about having a bigger purpose for the sake of it.

AUDIENCE MAPPING

Audience mapping can seem a bit technical and jargony to people who are unfamiliar with the concept. But it really doesn't have to be; it's a technique we've borrowed from our big-agency backgrounds to help small businesses.

What is audience mapping?

Audience mapping is about reaching the right people. It is about knowing their likes and dislikes, what language they use and what their problems are. It helps you to refine the more technical demographics such as country, region, gender, age groups, preferences or consumer insights. To start, you could look at the insights of your business and personal profiles on social media to give you a snapshot of the customer insight information available to you, which will help to reduce the wider audience circle.

Why do we need to do audience mapping?

Knowing your audience is one of the most fundamental parts of your brand strategy. On the basic customer journey, we have the first step of awareness and interest. This is where it's about becoming visible to a target audience. Then, you need to maintain that interest and develop that relationship. Lastly, after your customers have purchased, your brand has to switch to maintaining that relationship. Your audience will need different messaging and content at different times of this customer journey, but what it will also require is an aligned and well-thought-through brand at all these touchpoints.

If you are just starting out and taking your time to build your product or service, it's not necessarily a case of waiting until it's ready to do this work. In fact, some of the most successful businesses start focusing on audience engagement and community way ahead of the launch. This means that when it does come to getting word out there about your products you already have a warmed-up audience.

For the next exercise, we are going to look at the following characteristics:

- *Demographics*: this is the more statistical/factual information about your audience. It can include their age, geographic location or gender.
- *Psychographics*: this is more about your audience's behaviour and likes/dislikes. This is important for helping you create content that resonates in the places your audience is playing.
- *Business challenges*: you need to be an expert in what your customers' problems are so that you can ensure your brand, marketing and PR collateral addresses their needs.

AUDIENCE MAPPING

Make notes on your audience in your playbook or notebook. Consider these demographic characteristics:

- How old are your customers? What is the gender split?
- How much do they earn?
- Where do they live?
- Where do they shop?

Now consider these psychographic characteristics:

- What do your customers believe in?
- What do they care about?
- What do they like to do in their free time?
- What subscriptions do they have? Netflix/Spotify/Medium/Duolingo?
- Where do they learn: reading, videos, audio?

And lastly, think about their current business:

- What are their top three business problems?
- If they could fix one thing in their business, what would it be?
- If money was no issue, what would they invest in next for their business?

AUDIENCE MAPPING

35 / Years old / **44**

 75%

25%

££
up to VAT threshold

 Urban: cities and suburbs

 Fast fashion

 aspire to buy eco-friendly, sustainable and vegan

 Netflix Spotify Medium

EMPOWERMENT ENTREPRENEURSHIP IMPACT

 Traditional news **30%**

 Social media and blog **70%**

Tips

- Do you already have two to three previous clients who are your perfect customer? Could you invite them for a lunch/coffee to get to understand their business better?
- Are you making the most of the assets you already have? You probably already have a lot of analytics on your audience without realizing – make sure you check your insights across your social media channels.

- Can you create an incentivized Google form (e.g. win a voucher or a one-to-one session with you) as a way to encourage data gathering to help form your strategy?
- There are plenty of freelance brand strategists who can help with this if you get really stuck.

BRAND BEHAVIOUR

What does 'behaviour' mean when we talk about a brand? Let's go back to our fiction book example. In our fiction book, we might introduce a character. We might describe him like this: 'Here is Obi. He is 25, he likes music, he is a student at Manchester University, he likes football and plays twice a week with his friends, he likes sweet food not sour.'

Through all of these things, we start creating a world around his persona. Then, once we know about him, we start creating an impression of patterns about how Obi behaves, which gives us a clear snapshot of who Obi is. When this is done well, and we read a brilliant book, we can *picture* the characters described. We begin to know these made-up people so well that we can predict their next movements and we know exactly who they are – when they are happy, when they are kind or when they are sad.

For your brand, this means going beyond the *thinking*. Just like for our fictional Obi character, we need to consider not only what the theories are, but how you want to be perceived and think in advance how you want to react in different situations.

How does my business act on social media? How do we talk in our advertising? What type of content do we create?

Every time we take an action, what is the stance we take on society? What do we stand for? Once you have done all of the planning, it's important to think about your business in the real-life situations. How do you behave?

Some people call this a manifesto or a pledge. It is often written as a booklet. We see it a lot in politics, where political parties pull together a brochure on their manifesto. It is important because it is going to help inform you, your company and your employees – but more importantly, it is going to help shape in a tangible way how you act, react and behave.

ACTIVITY

BRAND BEHAVIOUR

Forget your competitors for now. This activity is all about you, and the way you want to do business. We want your audience to fall in love with you and no one else.

Aim for a small collection of short sentences. Start each sentence with, e.g. We believe/I do/I agree.

You can write as many as you want, but make sure you have a set of rules. In the 'How We Behave' section of the playbook we have left a blank box for you to complete. If you need a prompt to get started, then have a look at the following questions and answer the ones that apply to your business:

- What are the two to three key characteristics or points of differentiation of your product or service? Using these, complete the following sentence:
  - ○ 'We/I believe in…'

- Pledge how you intend to back up this belief with action by completing the following sentence:
  o 'We/I will always…'

- What are the two to three ways in which you operate that make you stand out in your market? Using these, complete the following sentence:
  o 'We/I believe in…'

- Pledge how you intend to back up this belief with action by completing the following sentence:
  o 'We/I will always…'

- What are the two to three purposes or social impact goals that you care about (e.g. climate change, diversity, homelessness, etc.)? Using these, complete the following sentence:
  o 'We/I believe in…'

- Pledge how you intend to back up this belief with action by completing the following sentence:
  o 'We/I will always…'

EXAMPLE

BRAND BEHAVIOUR

YOKO (You're Only Kids Once) is a parenting platform on a mission to make all parents' lives easier and brighter while shaking up the outdated stereotypes and portrayal of parenting and family life around the world.

Here is their manifesto, using the 'we believe/we will' model:

We believe in a world that sees the person first and the parent second. One that celebrates and welcomes all family set-ups, dreams and ambitions. A world that encourages and supports people to raise the bar while they raise their families. You're Only Kids Once, and life is short, so make every moment count. It takes a village; we are yours.

Here's another made-up example from a product perspective. Say your point of differentiation is that you are only using local suppliers. In that case, your statements could be: 'We believe in supporting local economic growth and celebrating a nation of proud and talented craftspeople. We will only work with…'

Tips

- This is not about creating a statement for public consumption; this is about really asserting what it is you believe in.
- If there are several stakeholders in your company, do this task individually and then discuss it together to find your crossover.
- Be as bold as you can be; if you leave space for whimsical statements then there is too much opportunity for interpretation.

HACK

Have your brand behaviour written down as a checklist. When approached by others for brand partnerships, press opportunities or any type of collaboration, make sure they are not in conflict with your brand behaviour. They don't have to be a direct match, but your core concepts should be the same.

CHAPTER SUMMARY

Ok, well done for getting this far. If you have successfully completed all of the activities in the playbook, then *really* well done! You have now set the brand strategy and created brilliant foundations for the building blocks of your brand house.

As a recap, you should now:

- have an idea about your market, competitive set and place;
- know your values and what you are about;
- understand your business mission;
- be well on your way to greater business success because you know your purpose.

We can now start to create what your brand building is going to look like. This is the really exciting part where we get a bit more meat on the bones – so come on, let's crack on already!

CHAPTER 2

HOW TO BUILD YOUR BRAND TOOLKIT

HELL YES OR HELL NO!

Hadrien Châtelet

In Chapter 1, we went through the strategic work that needs to underpin your brand and your business. In this section, we are grabbing all the equipment and resources we need to bring our concept to life visually.

VISUAL BRANDING

Now, this book is not trying to teach or mentor the next wave of award-winning graphic designers. But the visual stuff is obviously an important part of building your brand – even though it's not the main part – so it's clear that you will need to understand the graphic elements that can be used to create emotion and convey storytelling. Fear not – we'll go through the main visual branding elements you need to learn now.

MOOD BOARD

The hardest part you will likely face when considering the visual parts of your brand is how to know what looks good. What colours work? How do you find the best style?

In our experience, many small business leaders don't feel confident enough in how to choose colours, let alone other visual elements – it's scary, and it is a bit of an unknown. People often feel as if there is an insurmountable gap between what they are capable of designing and what they want their visual brand to be. It can be so frustrating to have all these ideas – and no clue how to convey them!

But don't panic! Even the most amazing creative designers don't just pluck ideas out of thin air. They get inspired, they think, try things and look around. More often than not, it's their surroundings that inspire them. And the same is true for you: you can't create anything from thin air, nobody can! You *can* get inspired by your surroundings. A really key way to do this, and something that I see used by many strong and powerful brands, is creating a mood board. This is the most important step in creating your visual brand.

There are often two opposite reactions to being asked to put together a mood board: people either think, 'Great! This is really easy, let me just slap some stuff together!' Or they freeze up and don't have a clue where to start. Neither reaction is likely to be all that helpful to you – so don't worry, we're going to go through some step-by-step ideas to help!

ACTIVITY

MOOD BOARD

First, choose how you will create your mood board. It can be an old-fashioned collage with scissors, paper and glue, if that's what fits you best. I enjoy doing it in a tactile way because it gets me away from a digital screen and forces me to look hard around me. Weekend supplements of national newspapers are good for this exercise because they often play with different designs, colours and fonts. It also really makes me take a good look at what is happening around me. I might use song lyrics or album covers to bring in a music element.

Many people are time poor and they need to make the process as easy as possible; for this you could use software like Keynote or PowerPoint. Simply search Google Images for the type of content that resonates with you and drag and drop. Or I love a good Pinterest board. You can collect a few different boards for the topics below or just create one main board to incorporate all of the elements we suggest.

Sort your mood board into sections, or create a checklist, to make sure you end up with everything you will need for your visual brand. You will want to consider some or all of the below:

- fonts
- colours
- layouts
- images
- moving images
- sounds
- product packaging
- social media assets

Once you have decided *how* you're going to create your brand mood board, you then have to decide *what* is going to go on it.

From Hadrien's experience, he runs through each of the elements above and takes the following steps when sourcing inspiration:

- *Emotion.* Start with emotions – maybe there is a colour that makes you feel really good? Or a sense that a certain font is perfect for you, because you like the angle and the impression of boldness and expertise? What about songs? How do you want your brand to make people feel – and what can you put on your mood board that evokes that feeling?
- *Preview.* When you start materializing your ideas, you will quickly get a preview of your brand. This is

going to help get you into the headspace of what your brand could look like.

- *Am I right?* Once you have a preview, you can reflect and consider whether what you have so far works well, or not. When you see it on paper, with all of your ideas, does it look a bit too much, or does it fit together? Think about the competitor analysis you did in Chapter 1. How do the story you are telling, and the visual you are creating, match up? Maybe your main competitor has a really interesting use of colour and font – do you need to refine your colour or font so that it's not too similar to theirs?

Tips

- You can either pull the ideas from online or you can cut images out of magazines – whatever works best for you.
- Be precise. Maybe you like green, for example, but there are so many different variations of green, all of which can convey a slightly different feeling. Take the time to research online: try Pinterest, Google Images or the Behance Network, look at the work of different designers and different sources like wallpaper, logos, photographs – try to narrow down the *exact* shade that's right for you.
- You may want to consider creating different mood boards for different spaces (e.g. one main one, one for Instagram, one for your blog… and so on). When it comes to creating these assets later on, you will already have reference points.

EXAMPLE

TYPEFACE MOOD BOARD

LAYOUT MOOD BOARD

IMAGERY MOOD BOARD

COLOUR MOOD BOARD

COLOURS

Colours are fascinating. There is so much to learn about colours; they are everywhere and have been used for years to affect human behaviour. We're not talking about branding or design here: colour has an impact on the actions people take in everyday life, at a functional and basic level. Think about traffic lights, for example. Pretty much universally, we know that red means stop, green means go and yellow is in between. We take it for granted, but it's applied everywhere. Then there are less concrete associations: green might make you feel like earth, for example, because the green you see around you is usually trees, grass, leaves and what you can see in nature.

Keep in mind though, that not all of these associations are universal. In the UK, for example, the colour red can often have negative connotations – red means stop, red is blood, red is danger. In Japanese culture, however, red means hope and is a positive colour.

Colours can help to differentiate you from your competitors but also to be more memorable.

Quick note: Psychologists have found that using colours enhances an individual's visual memory. When tested, people remembered the image of a blue sky more than a green sky.[3] With that in mind, let's review how each colour can make us feel and select the most relevant and memorable for your brand.

---

[3] www.scientificamerican.com/article/color-images-more-memorab/.

Each tone of each colour will make you feel and react in a certain way. The more brands use the right colours to evoke the right emotions, the more we remember them. The following is a quick cheat sheet for the different feelings that can be associated with different colours:

RED

We know that just by looking at the colour red, your blood pressure rises and your heart beats faster. Red – in its positive associations – is exciting, youthful, bold and vibrant. It helps you move forward; it is energetic. Red is an appetite enhancer; it makes you want to consume – just like insects and birds are attracted to red flowers. It's often used by food brands, innovative brands or fashion brands.[4]
Brand examples: Miso Tasty, MoneyMedic, UnderPinned, TedX.

ORANGE

Orange is basically yellow, with a bit of the intensity of red. It makes you feel cheerful, friendly, confident, free, energetic but calm; it brings the idea of possibility and discovery. We often see orange used by children's brands and communication brands.
Brand examples: The Inspiration Space, Headspace, Straight Talk Talent, High Fifteen.

---

[4] www.psychologistworld.com/perception/color.

YELLOW

Yellow evokes optimism, fun, clarity, warmth and is welcoming. Yellow is a colour that's engaging, welcoming and pleasing to look at. It is often used by sweet food brands like candies, soda or cereals. It's the feel-good feeling.
Brand examples: Sisters in Business, I am Super Sapien, Trint, I Like Networking.

GREEN

Green is extremely peaceful, earthy, eco-friendly, respectable. Many brands adopt green to try to make you feel that they are a better, more responsible or eco-friendly business.
Brand examples: Slick Pivot, BBC Woman's Hour, WA Green London.

BLUE

Blue is quiet, balance and calm. It gives you the feeling of stability and expertise, trust and wisdom. Lots of brands use blue to instil strength. But unlike red and yellow, bright blue unconsciously puts us off eating, like a blue frog who scares predators with its colour.
Brand examples: HaBox uk, Pencil Me In Shop, Yoko Global, English 4 French.

PURPLE

The colour purple speaks of creativity, youth and thinking outside the box. Depending on the shade, purple is the child of blue, yellow and red – so you can think of it as a bit of all of those feelings, only less intensive. It's calm and positive.
Brand examples: Black Unicorn, Rainchq, Purple Bricks.

GREY

Grey is calm, neutral, respectable and trusted. In a way, when you use grey, it's as if you are stepping back to make space for the consumer, the content, the imagination or the product. Grey signals respect and privacy.
Brand examples: Apple, Pet Pawtraits, Bird & Pup, Alush.

RAINBOW

Many brands use all the colours to represent diversity and positivity. Using a wide range of colours shows your intention to speak to all, and creates a range of emotions. It's often used by network or media brands and universities.
Brand examples: House Gospel Choir, Doing It for The Kids, Colour Celebrations.

Final thought on colours: Knowing the general feeling or emotion that a colour will evoke in your consumer is a huge advantage. Don't overthink it, though – make sure to not get yourself stuck into a purely rational and linear interpretation of colour. Trust your gut and emotions to choose the right colour for your brand.

ACTIVITY

COLOUR

This is a simple three-step process to nail your colour palette.

1. *Choose your main colour.* You also need to choose the proportion of use for this main colour – ideally, it should be about 60% to 70% of all the colours that you use. Remember, be precise – play around with the tone and shade of the colour until you get your 'Got it!' moment.
2. *Choose your secondary colour* (i.e. the contrast colour). In any design or format you do for your brand, wherever the main colour appears, the secondary colour has to contrast. For example, if you want to do an Instagram post with text over your main colour, the text needs to be readable – it wouldn't work if the text was too similar a shade to the background. Here's a quick technique to help you choose your contrasting colour: draw a square using PowerPoint, Keynote or Canva (or whatever software you're happy using). Make it a nice big square in your main brand colour. Then type on top and try out different text colours, until you find the combination that feels strong, has impact and stands out.

3. *Choose your neutral colour.* For this, it's important to choose a pastel tone like light grey or blue. It needs to be a tone that's quite close to white, so it can neutralize your two contrasting colours. That way, if you need to do something that is calm, or light, or has a softer feel to it, you have the right colour lined up.

EXAMPLE

COLOUR

I'm not going to lie to you: it's pretty hard to present examples of colour in branding in a black and white book so please head to our playbook where we have plenty of examples or look at Hadrien's profile on Pinterest for colour boards (search 'Hadrien Châtelet' on Pinterest).

Tips

- Use the colour psychology guide to help you, but don't think of it as a rulebook: ultimately, your colour needs to convey your emotion. You are 90% on the money if it feels exactly how you want it to feel!
- When you tweak a colour, it can change the meaning (e.g. a bright yellow has a different feeling to a mustard or a lemon shade). Trust your gut.
- Don't overdo it – it's very easy to go overboard, especially if you're a colour enthusiast, but it's really hard to make more than a few colours work together.
- Use https://colourcontrast.cc/ to test that your main and secondary colours have enough contrast.

HACK

Check out colours.cafe on Instagram for a huge selection of ready-made colour palettes or head to canva.com, create an account and log in. Under the heading 'Brand Kit', not only can you upload the content we create in this chapter but if you are really struggling for inspiration you can look at the trending colour palette under 'Add and Discover Colour Palettes' as a starting point, but be mindful that your brand isn't a trend.

FONTS

Type – the letters a brand uses – is one of the oldest forms of branding. One of the earliest recordings we have of branding being used were farmers marking their cattle with initials to say 'this cow is mine'. Think about our signatures, too – we are inadvertently using our own personal branding stamp with our signature! In many ways, it is who we are – that's how important type is.

The style of letters you choose to use is known as the font – when combined with rules about the size and spacing, you call the resulting lettering style a typeface. Your font, or typeface, is actually one of the biggest parts of your brand, and it can be the least expensive way to buy your own piece of visual branding. For less than £100, you can spend time learning about and choosing a font that really helps you to stand out. There is nothing wrong with Helvetica, for example – but it is very well known so it won't be unique to your brand. Of course, while some customers are super passionate and fascinated about fonts, for others it's not something they have ever even thought of – but when you start looking around you, fonts are absolutely everywhere!

COMMON TYPEFACE CATEGORIES

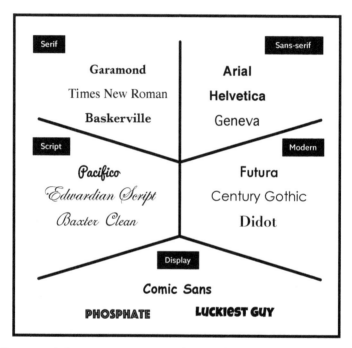

Micro activity: Next time you leave the house, have a look at the street signs, shop fronts, billboards, bus stop posters or even the different types of font used on leaflets, the sides of lorries or vans.

HACK

Typeface is the earliest and easiest way for people to tell that you have a brand. If right now you don't have a brand, the easiest, most affordable and best place to start is with your font.

Font characteristics and terminology

Font is a complex world, but we are here to help you navigate it. Just like colours, all fonts typically make you feel a certain way.

There are five major categories when you're looking at different fonts:

1. **Serif.** 'Serif' is the name we give to the little feet that letters in this category have. With the little feet, serif fonts are the classical old type that you have in the first version of Word, such as Times New Roman and other similar fonts; it looks a bit classic, a bit old-school and formal. Often used to signify expertise, it feels serious. These fonts can also be known as slabs.

- *Example*: *Monocle Magazine* (print and online entrepreneur lifestyle magazine).
It's really common for traditional magazines or newspapers to use a serif font, like *Monocle*. It gives a sense of longevity and seriousness, it makes you think about traditional and trusted older news outlets like *The Times* and this is exactly what *Monocle* wants you to feel – that it's a publication you can trust with reliable and serious information.

MONOCLE

2. **Sans serif.** 'Sans' in French means 'without', so this means without the serif (the little feet). When you remove these, the letters become clean and strict. Still classical, the size and spacing follow precise guidelines. These fonts make you feel calm and balanced but

without the traditional feeling – a pinch more modern. Typically, you might see a sans serif font in a business book. In this book we are using Avenir from the sans serif family. For the 1 in 10 of the population who are dyslexic, a sans serif font is a good choice; because they are often plain, evenly spaced and don't have any hooks on the end of the letters, they don't cause as much distraction. Think **Arial**, Century Gothic or **Verdana,** for example.[5]

- *Example*: UnderPinned – a one-stop career management platform for freelancers and a vibrant community platform for freelancers to grow and learn. Their goal is to attract freelancers from every discipline and background. UnderPinned provides service, community events and training. The usage of a sans serif typeface is to ensure that the audience can see themselves in this brand/logo due to its neutral visual aspect, but it also brings a feeling of expertise and trust. It is a simple and clear logo. In this situation 'less is more' is the perfect fit.

ᒐ UnderPinned

3. **Script.** This feels like it has been written by hand. It covers all the fonts that look like old handwriting. It can feel a bit old-school, but it is definitely approachable because it looks like someone has actually written it, so it feels personal.

---

[5] www.dyslexic.com/blog/quick-guide-making-content-accessible/.

- *Example*: Bliss Wine
  Bliss is a wine company based in South America targeting a female audience. It uses a lovely, loose, italic handwritten script style typeface that conveys an idea of both quality and accessibility. This tells us that this wine is for all – it is like your best friend has chosen the wine and then written a friendly message on the bottle before giving it to you.

4. **Modern.** These fonts can come in different variations, and is a much looser category than the others. They are usually still quite classical, but without the proportions that have been set in stone. Modern fonts make you feel forward-thinking and futuristic. They're quite often seen in technology like apps and websites.

- *Example*: Peddlers Gin
  In this example the font used is really close to a sans serif typeface but yet the weight and roundness of the letters give it a more modern and gentle feel. It gives the brand a twist of creativity and approachability without losing the feel of quality.

PEDDLERS GIN Cº

5. **Display or decorative.** This is a big variety of fonts with a particularly decorative look and shape. Perhaps this means strong handwriting, or it could be a font using just circular shapes. The emotion evoked here will obviously change a lot, depending on the type used, but a font like this can make you feel quite creative.

– *Example*: Leafage
   We mention Leafage later in the logo section but we also wanted to show them here as an example of display typeface. You might be thinking that it's a serif typeface. Well, you are right! To confuse matters it is based on a serif typeface, but the letters themselves have been transformed. There have been changes of proportion to create a more unique and modern feel. For example, the letter 'e' is circular with a generous curve downwards and the letter 'a' has an exaggerated belly. All together this makes us feel that it is a modern, stylish and beautiful brand.

Leafage

Apart from the categories, there is also the weight of your font to consider. The weight of the font is about the thickness of the letters. You can go from extra thin all the way up to knockout (which is the boldest it can be).

FONT FAMILY

Hello I am:

Gill Sans light
Gill Sans light italic
Gill Sans regular
Gill Sans regular italic
Gill Sans semi-bold
Gill Sans semi-bold italic
Gill Sans bold
Gill Sans bold italic
Gill Sans extra-bold

When you group all the weights of a font together, it's called a family.

So thinking of the 'Gill Sans' family, the fonts you have are: Gill Sans light, Gill Sans regular, Gill Sans bold, Gill Sans extra-bold, and so on. Usually, when you purchase a font, you have the option to buy the font family.

If you want to be a bit more advanced you can also look at font contrast. When a letter has the same width everywhere it has zero contrast. A high-contrast font is when the letters are thicker and thinner in different parts.

FONT CONTRAST

a	a
Zero contrast	High contrast

Rounded fonts are where the ends of the letters aren't straight: probably the most famous example is Comic Sans. If you want to go down a font rabbit hole here you might want to Google 'Comic Sans jokes'.

Alongside these characteristics are two more variables:

1. *Kerning* – the space between each letter. If you reduce the kerning it can make it feel more condensed. More spacing between each letter will make it feel calmer and a bit more stable.
2. *Leading* (pronounced 'ledding') – the spacing between each line. It is called 'leading' because originally in the printing presses they would use a thin piece of lead to get a thin line between each line.

Depending on how you use the different characteristics and variables, it can really change the mood and feel of the font. It can go from cuddly to calm or expert – anything you want really. Work with the weight, height, kerning and capitalization to create your emotion. Fine-tuning these can create a different story.

Now we have learnt about the different types of characteristics and variations, it's time to think about the uses of your fonts. Some fonts may be perfect to use for a header, title, masthead or even a logo, but be absolutely terrible to use for long copy. Imagine if this whole book was written using Desdemona – IT WOULD BE REALLY HARD TO READ.

With all the many small ways to customize and tweak your fonts, it is important that you put the functionality before anything. Although it is the font's job to evoke a certain emotion, it also has to have the characteristics of the usage you want it to have. When you are choosing your fonts, make sure that they spark the feeling that you want – but also make sure they are useful and fit for purpose. I would recommend that for long-form text, you pick something from the serif or sans serif family. But if you need something for presentations or headings, you need to go eye-catching.

This means you need to be selecting at least two fonts. Just like we had a main and a contrasting colour, we need to select a primary and a secondary font – as well as a potential third font, which is what you use for body copy (the bulk of all your written materials).

FONTS

In the playbook, or your own workbook, find and note down three fonts.

1. *Primary font.* First, pick something for the headers of your campaign, for your presentation, the main font for your slide. This should convey one of the top of your values from the values exercise we did in

Chapter 1. Start with the values you created earlier, and look at fonts from the font families that match who you are.

2. *Secondary font.* Now choose another font. This is your secondary font – we need to make sure this contrasts with your primary font. It's not like with colours where we can visually see the contrast. We are talking about different and complementary characteristics. If they are too similar, you may as well just stick with one; plus, if they are too similar, it will look strange, like you've made a mistake instead of a deliberate choice. You need to make sure you pick one that talks and challenges and stands out from the first one. They should talk to each other and with each other, like instruments in an orchestra. Ideally, it needs to be from an alternative grouping in our font house – so if you went serif for your main font, now you need to go sans serif.

3. *Body copy/third font.* Now you want a font that is easy to read. Pick something that is regular, light or medium with good variation of spacing. Make sure it feels right and that it isn't too creative!

Tips

- The best places to find free fonts are www.canva.com or www.fonts.google.com.
- Our favourite paid-for fonts are available at www.creativemarket.com or www.myfonts.com.
- Choose different fonts for different functionalities and make sure your pairings contrast.
- This is the first way to define your brand easily, so if you only have a small budget for branding, invest it in a font.
- Don't forget the functionality of the font – make sure it is readable when you use it out in the wild!

GRAPHICS, ILLUSTRATIONS AND IMAGES

In this section, we are talking specifically about images you use to represent your brand that fall outside of the obvious product or service that you offer. The reason that we need to create an image bank is because your job in terms of branding yourself is not to be selling your product all the time; you're not just selling one product, you're selling a *lifestyle*. We will talk more about personal branding imagery and photography in Chapter 3.

HACK

But why do we even need to be visual? Sara Dalrymple, a sales and visibility expert, gives us her top five ways that being visual can help in your business:

1. Showing compelling visual images is the fastest way to give your clients what they are looking for.

2. It's an easy tool to find and nurture common ground by allowing you to lead – use your personality to promote your product or service.

3. You can really create the atmosphere and experience that you want your clients to have.

4. Hate selling? For those of us who find selling cringey, visibility facilitates self-selection.

5. It has never been easier to show up for your business online or to find a way to do so that matches your personality.

Colours, fonts and accessibility

Regretfully it wasn't until a colour-blind person let me know that they couldn't read my website that I really started to pay attention to colours and fonts. Colour-blindness or colour-vision deficiency (CVD) could affect up to 8 of every 100 users that come to your website. So it's definitely worth considering the user experience for all of your visitors.[6]

Just before you hit print on your final designs, I would just do a quick check that you have made your packaging as visually clear as possible to people who are visually impaired and test it on your website first. Be particularly mindful of links, infographics, maps and games.[7]

Use high-contrast colours (e.g. between the primary and secondary fonts you select). Sans serif typefaces in larger font sizes and larger shapes can really help to make your branding stand out. On your website, try to avoid lower-contrast colours and the following colour combinations that can be problematic for colour-blindness:

- red and black
- red and green
- green and brown
- blue and purple
- blue and grey
- green and grey
- green and black[8]

---

[6] https://usabilla.com/blog/how-to-design-for-color-blindness/.

[7] https://99designs.co.uk/blog/tips/designers-need-to-understand-color-blindness/.

[8] usabilla.com and accessibility.psu.edu.

HACK

Check out https://colororacle.org, which is a free colour-blindness simulator for Windows, Mac and Linux.

Visual storytelling

Small business owners often try to start to build a brand through visual storytelling without first doing the work outlined in Chapter 1. We have tried to help you think about what emotions and feelings you want to convey and who you want to show that to.

Graphics, illustrations and images are extremely efficient ways to bring your brand alive, as well as bringing a sense of uniqueness.

A well-chosen or well-designed pattern will be much more memorable than any long text explaining how amazing your product is – and memorability and connection are very much what we are after.

So where a plain colour background will convey one note or one single feeling, a pattern or graphic will be able to deliver a more in-depth message through not only the colour(s) but by the shapes (angular, rounded, fine, fat, tall) and the style (hand-drawn, flat vector, 3D, playful, etc.).

But how do we create emotions? Well, we've started with our colours and fonts, but emotion, story and images are linked. Therefore, choosing the right images for your brand is about understanding how you can make the images work for your own narrative.

Image composition

Understanding image composition will help you to know what sort of story an image can convey. Some images are more powerful because of their composition. For example, let's take the famous image of the Last Supper by Leonardo DaVinci. If you have no idea who the people in the picture are or what is happening, you can quite quickly gauge who is the most important. The person in the middle wearing two colours is clearly the person who stands out. To back this up, all of the lines of construction and perspective and the horizon and corners of the room are pointing to him. The back of the room is a square that pulls us into the middle and even the horizontal line of the table pulls us into the middle space. Moreover, the lines of the ceiling draw into the central figure and the key figure is right in the middle. We therefore then know that something is happening and the person in the middle is a big deal.

EXAMPLE

IMAGE COMPOSITION

Geometrically speaking, the triangle is the most balanced shape you can find – think about a photographer putting the tallest person in the middle of a three-person group to create a triangle effect. Even in a one-person portrait, your own head and shoulders create a triangle! When you are thinking about choosing images, think about the construction and what it is saying.

EXAMPLE

IMAGE DOS AND DON'TS

DO

DON'T

DO

DON'T

Illustrations

Original illustrations can be extremely powerful in telling your story and helping your target audience get lost in the world of your brand. If you have limited budget and time, it can be the best way to create a complex and precise world or vision in a way that photos and video perhaps can't.

It can also be a way to give a unique, approachable and friendly touch to your brand. When well put together, a good set of illustrations can make a brand feel alive. The choice of style and message is limitless, so it really is a great opportunity for a small business owner to make their business stand out from the crowd.

Here are some things to consider if you choose to go down the illustration route:

- If you buy a stock illustration, make sure that it doesn't look too standard or common. Remember, the illustration needs to help you to stand alone and create your own world.
- An illustration can easily look unprofessional or childish, so whether you work with an illustrator or buy it, make sure it looks the part.
- If you work with an illustrator, take the time to look for one whose style is perfect for you, and make sure they are familiar with your brand strategy before they start the work.
- Always credit the illustrator when using their material and make sure you have the correct legal rights for different usage.

ILLUSTRATION

Bond was a series of business talks and conferences in New York. The illustrator Lisa Tegtmeier created a vibrant world composed of cool-looking and fresh women and men climbing on top of each other and talking to each other, all through the web page and posters. The style is simple and light, with three warm pastel colours. It makes you feel welcome, gives you a sense of community and creativity and, most importantly, it feels unique and premium.

Illustration by Lisa Tegtmeier, art director by Andy McMillan for bond.backerkit.com

Image bank

When you are building a brand or product, definitely think about building a bank of images – something between 5 and 50 – that you can use when you need to support or illustrate promotional content, social media or any type of material you need to create.

These images need to follow a consistent idea. Perhaps all of the images follow your brand story, or you can think of a slightly deeper concept. For example, if you are all about expertise and high quality, then you could think about a collection of high-end images that show the raw materials you use to create the product.

Here is a recap of the things to consider when choosing images for your image bank:

- The story of the image. Does this picture tell a clear story? Do I understand it?
- The layout. How is the picture put together? Is it well constructed, or do you need to crop it to make it work better? Where are the lines, and what are they pointing towards? Is it making you look at the centre, and is it working for the story you want to give to the picture? Is there a triangle or something else that makes you focus on the key point? We have put a good and a bad construction image in the playbook.
- Stock images. When you are starting out, you might not have the access, skills or budget to create your own photography or other graphic art. Choosing stock images from different websites is a really useful task to do; you can find free ones from websites such as Unsplash to help you to start. But be careful – when selecting images, you want to consider if it matches

the feeling you want to achieve, or if it feels cheesy, inauthentic, clichéd or too posed or fake (e.g. there are many comedic feeds around 'women laughing while eating salad', which sets a good barometer for images that feel a bit forced – have a Google).

ACTIVITY

GRAPHICS, ILLUSTRATIONS AND IMAGES

Using the playbook, select 5 to 10 images that will help represent your brand. Make sure they follow your stories and values, and ask yourself these questions:

- Is the story clear?
- Is the image relatable to your values and the story you want to give to your brand?
- Are your images well constructed? Is the main character or main event clear and on message?
- Do you need to search for a stock image? Does it feel real? Does it feel too staged?
- Does the image hit the level of quality and expertise you want to give?

EXAMPLE

IMAGE BANK

We worked with pivot coach Liz Ward, owner of Slick Pivot. Her brand story is all about providing an opportunity to people who are stuck in their life and who want a better view and to start a new fantastic journey. The emotions she needed to conjure were all about freedom, excitement, freshness and possibility. In helping her build her image bank, we only selected images of beautiful landscapes; images that were calling us for adventure. We didn't choose shots taken from above; we took shots that showed the central perspective and the road ahead. We wanted the viewer to feel that the adventure was aspirational but obtainable, and that anyone could get there. We wanted to convey that everything is possible, there are no barriers to your freedom or perspective. We didn't select the usual cheesy road path images that you can find anywhere, we chose shots that were realistic – as if we had gone to Scotland and taken the pictures ourselves. Take a look at the playbook to see what pictures we chose, or check out Liz's Instagram – her handle is @slickpivot.

Tips

- Hell yes or hell no! There should be no in-between in your imagery. Every time you use an image ask yourself if it represents who you are and what you

do. If you are unsure, then it's a no. It should make you unequivocally say, 'Hell yes!'
- Sharing a bad image can change your reputation, as it will alter people's perception of you. Be careful!
- You don't need to be too obvious and look too staged. As people and as consumers, we want things that feel authentic, so trust your gut and your emotions.
- Think of images to use for creating content, ads and blog posts.
- You are likely to need text and elements on top of many images. Think about embracing the negative – for example, could you use the sky or some white space to pop your text on?

Legal note

- You can't use someone else's image to sell your product or services without permission. There is a common practice on social media to share someone else's imagery with just a credit; in fact, you should be asking for their permission before you share – this is part of copyright law.
- Nearly every image created is protected by copyright, which gives the author the exclusive rights to use or reproduce their work. If you can't afford to pay for your imagery then here are a few of our favourite sites:
  ○ unsplash.com
  ○ pexels.com
  ○ canva.com
- Wherever you get your content from, make sure you check the terms and conditions before you use it (especially on free sites like those just mentioned).

LOGO

Here we are, it's time to talk about the logo design! We've come to this last on purpose – your logo is the pinnacle of your visual branding, it's the result of all the sums. To design a strong and memorable logo that conveys your brand message, you need to have perfected your brand strategy and know already the type of colour and typeface you will use.

As we have mentioned before, a logo *is not a brand*. Your logo is a symbol, an important piece of your brand that connects all the elements of your brand together. In some ways, you can think of it as your brand's signature. Every time you experience a brand, through the product, advertising, customer service interaction and so on, the logo will be there to unconsciously link all the dots together. This way your brain can create the brand world.

A logo on its own has no significant impact, but linked to all the brand elements, it becomes the most important piece of your puzzle to create brand recognition. In some cases – and especially with the rise of the social media influencer – you can build a strong brand without a logo. In this case, another element of your brand will take the place of the key visual link, like the actual person behind the brand or a recognizable typeface and colour combination.

Assuming you do want a logo, though, there are three main categories:

1. *Wordmark or logotype.* This is basically the name or initials of your brand written using a typeface that has impact and is – as much as possible – unique. It's simple, but can be very effective.

Example: Leafage
Leafage is a London-based terrarium brand which uses a distinct display typeface that blends playfulness with elegance.[9]

Leafage

2. *Symbol or icon.* This is a designed graphic or icon that is more or less abstract, and will represent your brand. A common mistake made by many designers will be to try to represent formally what the company does in a visual icon or symbol – like using a car for a car dealership. The problem with being too literal is that even if the consumer will understand your business faster, they will actually connect less because you won't have given them any emotion or uniqueness to connect with.

Example: Mean Mail
Mean Mail is an award-winning design-led greetings card company for those with a sarcastic sense of humour. Mean Mail's logo is two identical envelope icons. The simplicity and boldness of the lines make the strength of this mark. The duplication of the envelopes gives us the idea of communication between two parties – it is strong and impactful.

---

[9] Designed by Hannah Strickland. See www.weareleafage.com/.

3. *A combination of a logotype and a symbol.* This is when one or more letters are reinterpreted to create a symbol or a graphic to increase the uniqueness of the logo. This is usually very effective, and less time consuming than a full symbol logo.

   Example: allPaws by Green People UK
   This is a new pet care range for dogs with sensitive skin. The logo, created by Studio Kico, is composed of the full company name, with a dog paw print over the letter 'a'.[10]

allPaws

To sum up what you need to know about logo design, a logo should be unforgettable. It must stand out from your competition. A logo is usually the first piece of branding that your consumer will consciously connect with, and if it is not right it will forever give the wrong message. A logo must have the following characteristics:

- *Impactful*: the logo must stand out and create a long-lasting memory.
- *Unique*: a logo must represent your brand, and fit in with your brand strategy.
- *Timeless*: brand recognition takes time and effort to achieve; it can take several years before your audience fully remember you and have a clear brand picture. So you want to design a logo that will be as relevant in 10 years as it is now.

[10] See www.greenpeople.co.uk.

- *Clear*: whether the logo is a logotype or a symbol, or a combination, it must be easy to understand and read in any situation (e.g. from far away and close up, in digital form or print version, etc.).

A LOGO MUST BE

IMPACTFUL
UNIQUE
TIMELESS
CLEAR

Do it yourself or with a designer?

I can't stress enough that you should never see branding purely as an extra cost. I can say with conviction that branding is one of the best investments that you can make for your business. A large part of the future success of your company is based on your brand and your reputation, so why cut corners? Why not invest the time and effort and give yourself a real chance of success? Treat yourself like you would your best client.

Obviously, you can go to any website – I won't mention names! – and find any cheap designer that would be happy to design a logo for you. Maybe you even know someone who's a Photoshop enthusiast and is willing to help you. But the truth is that you are then more likely to spend a lot of time headshaking to reach a bad copy of what you are looking for… or a logo that looks fine now, but that in five months you realize is completely wrong and is actually pushing potential customers away. Work with a brand designer who will know the right process and questions to build the brand you will feel proud of, and that will attract the right audience to you (you can find out in Chapter 5 how to find, brief and work with a brand designer).

Tips

- Avoid using trending and quirky typefaces that will look dated in a few months.
- Invest in working with a brand designer who will build you a striking brand.
- A logo that says what is in the tin is good, but does not create long-lasting consumers – aim instead for a logo that creates emotion.

- Check out the legal and ethical considerations section later in this chapter for tips on the legalities of images and logos. Make sure before you hit publish on your brand that you are not infringing on any trademarks and do a Google Image logo check.

What you need to know

At the end of the design process, you must have a primary logo in full colour, a secondary logo or mark in full colour and a black and white version for print requirements.

You need to have all those logos in a vector format to be able to print them in large format as well as a pixel version for everyday use with an option to have a transparent background, called PNG.

OTHER BRANDING DECISIONS

Of course, not every decision you make will be about how your brand looks – there are some other important factors that will affect how you build your brand. Let's take a quick look at these now.

DIVERSITY AND INCLUSION

We are not diversity and inclusion (D&I) experts, but one of our bigger purposes as a business is to support equality.

We understand that being an advocate is more than just being vocal when racism, sexism, discrimination or bullying is reported in the media. While it's worthy of much more than a small section in our book, it didn't feel right to create a book about raising your brand without talking about our own individual responsibilities when building a brand.

It is easy to be guilty of creating a brand and content that only speaks to ourselves, and this can be a real problem – not just ethically, but for business too. At best, we could be directly excluding many prospects and turning our audience off; at worst, we could be risking cultural appropriation, causing huge offence or actually making it impossible for someone who has a visual impairment to even see our brand.

I can hand on heart tell you that the best money we have ever spent in training for the business was D&I training with Vanessa Belleau, founder of High Fifteen. It only scratched the surface of what we needed to know, because there is so much to cover. So for this book, we interviewed Vanessa, who is an expert in the D&I space as well as a qualified and experienced business strategist and executive coach to prompt your own thinking.

I would urge you to seek training and education for your own business but mostly to make sure that this is a consideration when building your brand right from the start, then think about how you can maintain that momentum every day.

Over to Vanessa!

Why do small businesses need to think about D&I when it comes to building their brand?
All small businesses need to think about how to bake D&I, also called diversity, equity and inclusion (DEI), in their

strategies because it matters. On top of being the right thing to do, it also creates a competitive relevance that cannot be denied.

It has been proven that businesses that put DEI at the core of their practices see significant results on their bottom line and brand salience, as they intentionally appeal to a wider audience and also tend to be more innovative and creative – two key qualities that tend to ensure brand relevance.

Small businesses need to think about DEI when building their brand because it really helps to segment an audience successfully and with a long-term vision. A very clear intersectional (i.e. the interconnected social aspects of individuals, taking into account gender identity, race, ethnicity, belief, sexual orientation, disability, etc.) approach is embraced when incorporating DEI from the start, which ultimately avoids 'othering' and devaluing any relevant potential buying customers, however small they might be.

When working with small businesses, what I realized is that many owners think about gender equity and take it seriously – partly thanks to the #MeToo movement. As a result, we have seen the proliferation of new businesses focusing on supporting women-led businesses and women founders.

The global outcry in 2020, highlighting the racial inequality that still exists in our society, showcased that business owners and founders do not truly understand what is at stake when it comes to the full impact that a focus on DEI has in our society. This moment in time really highlighted that there is a lot of work still to do – on both a personal and a business level.

Most small business owners generally care about DEI on a personal level – they understand that it is a vital topic for the advancement of our society and the right ethical stance to take. Yet, when thinking about their businesses, they often struggle to see how they can apply the same beliefs. They do not realize that they actually are in the best position to create diverse and inclusive strategies internally and externally.

This often stems from a real lack of understanding of what DEI is and what is really at stake in this conversation. D&I or DEI or even DIB (diversity, inclusion and belonging) should really be seen as business strategies and not a programme that is designed by a human resources (HR) team (which often only exists in bigger business structures).

DEI is about people, it is about all of us, it is about celebrating ourselves and the people around us. It is about widening and not narrowing perspectives and making sure that we understand that representation matters to more people than we think. It is about acknowledging that the world is global and multifaceted and that should be celebrated. It is not a chore or should not be seen as an add-on – something that we only tap into every so often.

In the words of Vernā Myers, 'Diversity is being invited to the party; inclusion is being asked to dance.'[11] Equity is about making sure that everyone can get to the party – independent of where they live, what budget they have for transport, clothing, etc. And belonging is being able to dance to music you love and like nobody is watching!

---

[11] www.vernamyers.com/2017/02/04/diversity-doesnt-stick-without-inclusion/.

I shall repeat myself here and state once more that I truly believe that small businesses are in the best position to create diverse and inclusive strategies internally and externally. Why? Because it matters to their customers and they can rethink their business foundations (values, purpose and mission) far quicker than bigger businesses. In only a few words: they are agile and can take more calculated risks faster than bigger businesses. They are truly in the best place possible as they can trial and test new things pretty fast, involve their customers and adapt their strategies on a daily basis if they need to, albeit this is not recommended.

In a nutshell, yes, there is a commercial business case for D&I/DEI but the most important motivation to get involved with D&I and bake it into business strategies for small businesses should be the moral compass that ultimately emphasizes their purpose and values and that should, ideally, be commercially as well as societally invaluable.

What are the biggest mistakes you see small businesses make when it comes to D&I and brand building?
Some of the biggest mistakes I have noticed are as follows:

- Small businesses thinking that they are too small to incorporate D&I in their DNA and ways of doing business *every day*. This is due to a lack of understanding of what D&I really is and how it can actually support business positioning and growth.
- Small businesses not understanding the real impact that not being diverse and inclusive has on their bottom line and future prospects – ultimately the need to appeal to a wider intersectional audience.
- Small businesses remaining silent on major societal issues and treating D&I as an afterthought rather

than a driving force of their business, somehow in the fear of not being political.

- Small business owners reducing D&I to people and staff when the right mindset is to believe that D&I is a business strategy.
- Small business owners not educating themselves on all topics relevant to their community, however diverse it is.
- Copying other businesses' initiatives without genuinely doing the work and not thinking about the real impact those initiatives have on marginalized groups – basically following a 'one-size-fits-all' approach.
- Starting something and stopping (i.e. not thinking about baking D&I as a long-term strategy and lacking consistency as well as vision).
- Feeling that they have no right to raise awareness on issues because they don't belong to any marginalized groups and/or experience hardship.

For an absolute beginner what does it mean to work on D&I in your business?
Working on D&I means working on creating or evolving a business into a proposition that appeals to an intersectional audience and, with that, remain competitive and cultivate relevant values such as collaboration, respect, leadership and vulnerability. It is not a bonus but a requirement.

This means that they need to do two key things:

1. Understand that this conversation and re-focus of strategy are necessary and that it will require self-awareness, reflection, vulnerability, curiosity and collaboration – five principles that I present to frame

this conversation. This process will kick-start by small business owners being open to confront their own biases – conscious and unconscious.

2. Look at the basics and review the foundations of their business:
–   *Business purpose*: WHY do they do what they do? Making sure to test it against the societal landscape.
–   *Audience*: review who they are impacting now and want to impact, influence and cater to in the future – review the data about their current clients, audience and/or community.
–   *Collaborators*: review who their network of collaborators is and see how it can be improved to reflect society at large and get similar inputs. Getting perspectives from people who are 'not like us' is key when baking in DEI as an everyday practice.
–   *Marketing/content*: review their ways of expressing themselves on social media, on their website and/or how they show up every day via images they choose to post, sources of information they quote, language they use – make it as inclusive as possible, etc.

Something that I recommend is that they focus on identifying areas that will help them refine their brand positioning through the lens of D&I and really push themselves outside of their comfort zone.

It is key for me to note that they should know that it is never too late to start incorporating DEI in a business. Yes, it is always best to start a business and make it as diverse and inclusive as possible, but 'better late than never' really applies in this conversation.

As the expert in this space, can you leave us with any takeaway tips on how small businesses with a limited budget can learn more about D&I?

- If you can't work with a D&I expert there are a lot of free resources and books that require a small up-front investment.
- LinkedIn provides D&I courses at a reasonable cost on their learning platform. Coursera and Open Learn are good platforms as well.
- *Forbes* and *Harvard Business Review* offer plenty of articles, and if you are more of a listener there are a bunch of podcasts available on this topic.
- Write a pledge – you don't have to share it with anyone but make yourself accountable to making progress one day at a time.

Any final notes you want to add Vanessa?
My best advice to small business owners is not to be afraid to make mistakes. Reach out to your network/the network of your network, be genuine, ask questions, be open and honest about your shortcomings and your will to learn and hope for great connections. Take risks – operate outside of your comfort zone.

EXAMPLE

As Vanessa notes, this isn't about watching what one business does and copying. So I would stress here that I wanted to share a few ways that we as a business are trying to implement D&I into the everyday to help spark ideas. We are far from perfect, so I was even nervous about putting ourselves forward as an example. I'm very aware that we are only scratching the surface. Part of that means the case studies and examples we included couldn't just be a tick-box exercise but people we already knew or were connected to. It highlighted to me while putting this book together just how much work we still need to do to expand our network and relationships with other marginalized groups. We are very much at the start of our journey and I hope it inspires you to take some action on yours too.

We still make mistakes but are open to learning from these failures to become a better business.

- *Events/partnerships.* We have previously said yes to hosting guest workshops or appearing on panels without thinking too much about the association. We are now taking extra due diligence to ask who else is on the panel, flagging if we think it is not representative and giving up our seat if required.
- *Social media.* We have started to consciously diversify our follower list. Clubhouse, for example, provides a real opportunity for us to be the minority in a room and listen and learn from experiences outside of our own. We have a list of key D&I dates and where relevant look to include them or talk about them on our social channels.
- *Images/illustrations.* Hadrien is building a more diverse roster of agency partners that we can collaborate with. He is also more mindful in the imagery he selects and presents back to clients. If their website/branding is full of people who are not representative he will flag it.
- *Newsletter.* In our monthly 'Hype Yourself' newsletter I am consciously thinking about who I include in the friends and family list.

- *Team meetings.* In our weekly team meeting we have a D&I chat each week to talk about what actions we are each doing individually to keep the momentum going. This has been key; it can be very easy to only react to obscene news stories, but talking about it weekly helps us to maintain the conversation. We continually find gaps and areas where we can improve and the weekly meeting keeps us accountable and moving forward.

LEGAL AND ETHICAL CONSIDERATIONS

One problem for small business owners when it comes to building your brand is that quite often people can miss or avoid sorting out any legal issues until it is too late. As small business owners we often tend to treat our business a bit like a medical problem, in that we don't actually seek preventative advice but only rush to see an expert once we have the symptoms of an impending legal flare-up. We wanted to flag some common pitfalls to watch out for.

For small business owners, getting affordable legal support is a real issue, particularly when it comes to protecting your brand and its assets. So, to help you, we have interviewed start-up and entrepreneur legal specialist Egbe Manton. Egbe set up Manton Legal during the global COVID-19 pandemic in 2020–2021, with more small business owners looking to pivot their services. Multiple business owners reported that they needed legal support but that law firms were too expensive for their budget. So they would download free contract templates and hope for the best! She knew that there was a better way for people building a brand.

Over to Egbe!

What are the biggest challenges small business owners face when it comes to getting legal protection for their business?
Knowing when to hire a legal expert – legally protecting your business is a specialist area and is not something that should be taken lightly. Legal experts are invaluable and can assist with everything from determining the most appropriate business structure to providing guidance on contracts, intellectual property (IP) and data protection requirements.

Affordability – legal support is sometimes seen as an expensive cost, but it could save you from making costly mistakes in your business. Traditionally, the only offering for small businesses were law firms that had large overheads and costs, and this was reflected in their fees. Times have changed and there are now different legal options for small businesses. These options include legal tech products, legal consultants and law firms.

Why is investing in legal support when building a brand important?
Given the tricky nature of building a brand, there are too many aspects that could go wrong. You should minimize this by seeking legal support not only at the start of your business but at each growth stage.

I know of businesses that have prepared to launch new products to the market and have invested in costly marketing campaigns, secured their website domains and incurred manufacturing costs. Then they found out that the relevant trademark for their brand had been taken years earlier by another company in the same trademark class they wished to apply for.

Had they invested in legal support they would have been aware of this prior to incurring costs.

What do you say to businesses starting out who have no budget when it comes to building their brand?
Start with the essentials – what are the key brand assets that you need to legally protect?

For example:

- Do you need to protect your business name via a trademark? This would prevent you from infringing someone else's trademark and would also ensure that third parties are unable to use an identical or similar name. It's a few hundred pounds to set up but could save you tens of thousands on legal fees.
- Do you know that your work may be protected via copyright? This is a legal right that protects your work and prohibits others from using it without your consent.

COPYRIGHT AND PLAGIARISM

In addition to the excellent guidance from Egbe, it is worth flagging that there are some copyright issues you need to be aware of when it comes to building your brand – especially when doing the visual work from the first part of this chapter.

In the UK, if you create a limited company this can just be your trading name and doesn't have to be the final name of your business. Consider a working title name if starting from scratch just so that it doesn't hold you back. If you use a brand or product name that is similar to another brand, particularly if you are working in the same field, then you could face a potential legal claim.

COPYRIGHT AND PLAGIARISM

- Start with a social media search to ensure that nobody else in the same field is using the exact same name. Note that this is not an exhaustive way to check as there could be larger companies with a brand in development, but this is a good first litmus test.
- In the UK, we have Companies House, but check the respective local market company registration site of the area you intend to operate in and do a name check.
- Again, in the UK we have the Intellectual Property Office (IPO), which is responsible for IP rights. A lot of companies register their brand as a trademark, so check your brand name here.
- Google 'brand name checker' for a local brand name search.

EXAMPLE

COPYRIGHT AND PLAGIARISM

Disclaimer: we don't want to inadvertently get ourselves into our own legal tangle so have not included a brand example here.

Tips

- Try the WIPO Global Brand database www.wipo.int, where you can upload an image or do an international name check.
- Use Google Reverse Image search via the Chrome browser to enter your logo or brand symbols to check they are not a trademark copy.
- It might only cost you a couple of hundred pounds to protect your brand but could cost tens of thousands to save it. Being a small business doesn't exclude us from big legal fees. Seriously consider registering your company name if you have not already.

Not illegal but not great

One of the common examples of plagiarism we see is where the font and colour palette are copied. Now this isn't technically illegal, but it's definitely unethical, so we just wanted to touch on why stealing someone else's font and brand colours, or any other brand work, isn't a great idea.

It's quite insulting to take the hard work and planning they have put into creating their own footprint. Take The Wern, for example: our font is on my first book, the website, brochures, and products, so when someone casually adopts the exact same font and colour palette for their Instagram, it starts to diminish my own messaging and work. Being inspired by someone's work is great – it is totally fine to want to have a similar brand identity to businesses that you relate to – but you need to be creating your own brand to reflect your own individual identity. Otherwise not only is it unethical, but it simply won't work as well for you!

Picking off your competitors' audience

Again, not illegal but casually a bit grim. Are you inadvertently following their ex-wife or parents? Being inspired by a competitor is one thing but if you start to get on their radar because you are following all of their friends, family and best customers, then it makes for bad practice. One of the perks of being a small business owner is we don't need to stoop to a bullying, big-business corporate mindset. The audience pool is huge; we don't need to swim in someone else's to be successful.

The one issue that I find the most disappointing is that the copyright and plagiarism issues that have affected the small business owners I know have mostly stemmed from people they themselves know. Often, people starting out who send cute messages about not knowing where to start and asking for recommendations about suppliers and contractors. For a lot of small business owners the research to find the right partner can take days and weeks, so actually these innocent questions can be quite troublesome. More often than not these are genuine messages from people starting out, but a minority are not. I'm pretty sure if you are reading this book you don't fall into this category. So let's turn our attention briefly to what you can do if this happens to you. Legally, again, there is little you can do to stop someone who wants to use or work with your suppliers, but you can get a contract in place with them to ensure that they can't reproduce your work or work with a competitor without your consent.

I want to reinforce that the majority of small business is good business, but don't wait until a legal challenge faces your brand to consider legal support. I'd highly recommend legal expert Shireen Smith's *Brand Tuned: The New Rules of Branding, Strategy and Intellectual Property* (2021), which expands more on branding law and IP.

EDITORIAL GUIDELINES

Doing all the work from the sections in Chapter 1 is going to help you with a very important part of your brand-building jigsaw puzzle: your tone of voice.

They way in which we speak to people is something that most people don't always connect with their brand; maybe if they think of it at all, it's assumed to be a part of the communications strategy. But your brand's tone of voice will appear in advertising, newsletters, packaging, social media, your website… everywhere! It's the verbal or written 'friendly face' that greets your customer at all touchpoints. For people who are not so keen on elevating their personal brand as part of their business, they can still bring their personality and ethos through in their editorial touchpoints.

For small businesses, nailing their tone of voice can be particularly important and therefore the job of writing the company blog, for example, can be outsourced to a content creator. We will talk more about the type of blog articles you can write in Chapter 3. Research by Hubspot shows that companies that blog generate 55% more web traffic, and 57% of businesses have also won a customer through their blog.[12]

Tone of voice is a crucial element of your brand building. In fact, we want to take this one step further – we recommend

---

[12] https://blog.hubspot.com/blog/tabid/6307/bid/29351/11-editorial-guidelines-every-business-blog-needs.aspx.

that you reframe your 'tone of voice' more formally as 'editorial guidelines'. This is a formalized and planned set of rules, guides and examples that govern everything created by your brand – the wording you use, how things are spelled, guidelines around swearing or violence... everything, down to which words need capital letters or not!

Creating your own set of editorial guidelines is handy not just for all your team and external freelance support to understand your business, but it can actually be an asset that helps drive long-term sales for your business. It will also help you form the basis for the personal branding work in your business, to be discussed in Chapter 3 – so although it may seem like a lot of detail for this part of the process, don't skip it.

ACTIVITY

EDITORIAL GUIDELINES

Before you begin this activity, it is essential that you have completed the activities in Chapter 1. If you don't have a solid grasp of your brand values, the competitors and your target audience, then you are going to struggle to think about how you speak to them. A full template is available as part of the playbook but included here is a checklist for you to think about.

- *Brand values*: review the brand values you created earlier in the chapter and write down what these are.
- *Types of content*: what are your content touchpoints? Website, newsletter, brochures, social media, workshops?
- *Tone of voice*: thinking about your brand values, what tone of voice do you want to use? Are you

educational, expert, fun, informative, chatty, confident, no-nonsense, ambivalent, opinionated?
- *Layout*: what formatting standards do you need to set out?
- *Primary font*: what are you using for your headlines?
- *Secondary font*: what are you using for your subheading?
- *Third font*: what are you using for body copy?
- How do you use *spacing/alignment* or any other layout notes for how you write?
- *Logos, photography and images*: create a 'dos and don'ts' list for how you use logos, images and photography within your copy.

BONUS ACTIVITY

EDITORIAL GUIDELINES

There are certain businesses that have catchphrases or marketing phrases that stick in your head. For example, Leafage has notes on its packaging such as, 'No garden? No problem!' or 'Don't kale my vibe'; while paper-goods social enterprise Who Gives a Crap uses messages such as, 'Not your average toilet paper' and 'Sit down for what you believe in'.

Think about how you could add additional phrasing that becomes associated with your product or service.

EDITORIAL GUIDELINES

The following is a snippet taken from Mailchimp, who are often cited in marketing blogs as a shining example of strong editorial guidelines. You can search for the full document online but we include an extract here:[13]

Voice and tone

One way we write empowering content is by being aware of our voice and our tone. This section explains the difference between voice and tone, and lays out the elements of each as they apply to Mailchimp.

What's the difference between voice and tone? Think of it this way: you have the same voice all the time, but your tone changes. You might use one tone when you're out to dinner with your closest friends, and a different tone when you're in a meeting with your boss.

Your tone also changes depending on the emotional state of the person you're addressing. You wouldn't want to use the same tone of voice with someone who's scared or upset as you would with someone who's laughing.

The same is true for Mailchimp. Our voice doesn't change much from day to day, but our tone changes all the time.

---

[13] Used with permission from https://styleguide.mailchimp.com/voice-and-tone/.

Voice

At Mailchimp, we've walked in our customers' shoes, and we know marketing technology is a minefield of confusing terminology. That's why we speak like the experienced and compassionate business partner we wish we'd had way back when.

We treat every hopeful brand seriously. We want to educate people without patronizing or confusing them.

Using offbeat humor and a conversational voice, we play with language to bring joy to their work. We prefer the subtle over the noisy, the wry over the farcical. We don't take ourselves too seriously.

Whether people know what they need from us or don't know the first thing about marketing, every word we say informs and encourages. We impart our expertise with clarity, empathy and wit.

All of this means that when we write copy:

- *We are plainspoken.* We understand the world our customers are living in – one muddled by hyperbolic language, upsells and over-promises. We strip all that away and value clarity above all. Because businesses come to Mailchimp to get to work, we avoid distractions like fluffy metaphors and cheap plays to emotion.
- *We are genuine.* We get small businesses because we were one not too long ago. That means we relate to customers' challenges and passions and speak to them in a familiar, warm and accessible way.

- *We are translators.* Only experts can make what's difficult look easy, and it's our job to demystify B2B-speak and actually educate.
- *Our humor is dry.* Our sense of humor is straight-faced, subtle and a touch eccentric. We're weird but not inappropriate, smart but not snobbish. We prefer winking to shouting. We're never condescending or exclusive – we always bring our customers in on the joke.

Tone

Mailchimp's tone is usually informal, but it's always more important to be clear than entertaining. When you're writing, consider the reader's state of mind. Are they relieved to be finished with a campaign? Are they confused and seeking our help on Twitter? Once you have an idea of their emotional state, you can adjust your tone accordingly.

Mailchimp has a sense of humor, so feel free to be funny when it's appropriate and when it comes naturally to you. But don't go out of your way to make a joke – forced humor can be worse than none at all. If you're unsure, keep a straight face.

Style tips

Here are a few key elements of writing Mailchimp's voice. For more, see the 'Grammar and Mechanics' section:

- *Active voice:* use active voice. Avoid passive voice.
- *Avoid slang and jargon:* write in plain English.
- *Write positively:* use positive language rather than negative language.

Tips

- Creating editorial guidelines will serve you in the long run. It is impossible to do everything yourself as a business owner, and when you require marketing, creative, content agency or freelance support, clear written guidelines will be essential.
- Don't feel constrained to what you create now – this may well evolve over time as you and your business evolve too.
- Think about bigger brands whose tone of voice you admire or have a Google of 'examples of top brand editorial guidelines' to find some cases online to help steer you. Some great ones include Monzo, BBC and Buffer.
- If you will be writing a lot of articles on thought leadership in your business then consider investing in the Associated Press Stylebook, which can help with grammar, punctuation and style.

CHAPTER SUMMARY

Well done, you have made it to the end of Chapter 2. We have now mastered the main bulk of the brand-building work. Before we move into the personal branding section in Chapter 3 we can tick off:

- *Mood board*: a brain dump of how you want to look and behave visually.
- *Colour*: selected your colour palette.
- *Fonts*: identified your key fonts and how you will use them.
- *Graphics, illustrations and images*: got to grips with the ways you can break up text and other visual elements with behaviour-enhancing techniques.

- *D&I*: some considerations to underpin our brand strategy.
- *Legal and ethical*: things you should get protected and some minefields to watch out for.
- *Editorial guidelines*: a good idea of how you want to behave in your communications.

Buckle up for Chapter 3. We still have to get to work a bit longer to look at how we can help hype your business using your personal brand.

PERSONAL BRAND

QUOTE

STOP SELLING AND START SHARING.

Lucy Werner

In Chapters 1 and 2 we focused on strategy and deep thinking to form the foundations of your brand. We are now going to look at how we can extend this even further by focusing on you, as one of the brand tools of your business. Let's start with why we need to bring your personal brand into this book at all.

In some ways, PR and brand/graphic design can be seen as completely different disciplines – but personal branding is the intersection where there is a lot of crossover. While we might come to it with different toolboxes, we are chipping away at the same problem.

For a lot of our British clients in particular there can be some stiff-upper-lip behaviour that makes us feel suitably awkward about sharing ourselves without being asked. There are three points on this I would like to make. First, the word 'personal' trips people up and it's hardly surprising. One of the definitions of 'personal' in the *Cambridge Dictionary* is 'private or relating to someone's private life'.[14] But let me be clear: personal branding doesn't mean revealing everything about your private life, your children, partner, pets or what your house looks like. It's just showing a bit of ankle.

Which leads me to the second takeaway. In this book, we are talking about your personal brand specifically to promote your business. It isn't about becoming an influencer, bizfluencer or 'famous', it's about becoming known as an expert and an extension of your business or the company you work for. We'll look more at this later on in the chapter, but there is a way that you can hype yourself and your business and still retain humility. In fact, being humble is a great quality for an entrepreneur or small business to have!

---

[14] https://dictionary.cambridge.org/dictionary/english/personal.

Whether you are loud or shy, an introvert or an extrovert, there is a fine balance in promoting your expertise, skills and journey. In this chapter, we're going to dig a bit deeper into why it is important to do this, and how you can achieve that special *je ne sais quoi*.

And last but not least, the chances are, if you are reading this, you are a small business owner. Therefore for you, there is almost certainly a bigger purpose to your business, as we have already seen. So if this is you, and you have a wider purpose than simply making sales, then bear this in mind: it is much easier to get your customers to understand your purpose when it comes from a person rather than a faceless brand. This is supported by research from the University of Oregon, which noted in a WARC report that 'consumers are more likely to support brands that use faces in their imagery because people have a fundamental need to form and sustain relationships'.[15] I'm not saying you need to go as far as slapping your face on your product or website – but if you do choose to do this, it doesn't have to be icky and fame-seeking.

DISCOVER YOUR PERSONAL BRAND

The most underused tool by a lot of small business owners is themselves.

---

[15] www.warc.com/newsandopinion/news/consumers-prefer-brands-with-faces-on-labels/39199.

LINK YOUR PERSONAL BRAND STRATEGY TO YOUR BUSINESS BRAND

All too often they are so focused 'in' the business that they forget to share the 'on' the business bits that connect with the audience. Rather than just raising your head up above the parapet when you need to sell something, we are going to talk through how we can build a personal brand strategy that links to your business brand.

I liken personal brand to thinking of yourself like a magazine. When your target audience is looking for a service, brand or product to work with, what are they looking for on the shelf, what sort of photos, colours, fonts appeal to them? What stories and topics help them to connect and engage?

This is why the work in Chapters 1 and 2 is so relevant for your brand. Take The Wern, for example. We have bright colours and, while we showcase expertise and knowledge, *fun* is a key component of the brand. If I started to give very plain looking talks, workshops or events it would be in gross conflict with my business and brand values.

In fact, when I show up online, I get to have fun with our brand and bring our business ethos to life. In a way, it actually helps me in hyping myself because I get to have fun and ignite my creativity when crafting ideas for posts.

DISCOVERING YOUR PERSONAL BRAND

Let's start with a litmus test: use someone else's computer or phone, or use a different search engine than your normal one (like DuckDuck Go, for example), and see what appears when a stranger Googles you. Or you could use someone else's machine so that the cookies and search preferences don't skew your results – you could also use incognito mode or clear your cookies and browser history.

- Note down the top three places that your name appears. Is it your website? Your own work?
- What do you need to change? What is surprising?
- How did this exercise make you feel?

For some people, this can be an uncomfortable exercise, particularly if done in a group, but it's worth any discomfort – it's an incredibly useful tool to see what the general public will see when searching for you.

It will help you to see if any particular collaborations are showing up high on your Google search. Maybe you collaborated with a similar business and co-created content, or perhaps you did a question and answer (Q & A) for a niche platform online that is showing up top. This will allow you to then refocus your promotional efforts back into those sites that are showing up at the top of your search engine optimization (SEO) search.

DISCOVERING YOUR PERSONAL BRAND

Tips

- Don't become narcissistic and Google yourself daily, but think about checking once a month or once a quarter, to see which links are working hard for you and your business.

- As you start to elevate your personal brand, you may receive invites and pitches – it's important to ensure that these fit your brand values.
- For a top line on how you are appearing on social media, check Google's social-searchers.com.
- Twitter performs really highly for images on a Google search (as does MySpace RIP). Consider posting a tweet with a recent image of yourself to get a more up-to-date headshot showing.
- A quick way to improve your position as an expert is to join quora.com and spend five minutes a day for a fortnight answering questions in your area of expertise.

DESIGNING YOUR PERSONAL BRAND

Whether you love him or find him irritating, Gary Vaynerchuk's quote, 'There is no reason to do anything other than act like a media company in today's digital age',[16] ties into the magazine format I like to teach people about using their personal brand. Rather than thinking of personal brand as something cringey, think about how as a small business owner you can act like you are your own micro-publication, and the content you put out is like a virtual magazine.

When you think of a lifestyle publication, they are often broken down into the following:

- news pages – items/services/events happening right now;
- features – wider trends, features with experts, long-form articles;

---

[16] www.garyvaynerchuk.com/media-company-mentality/.

- comment and opinion;
- imagery and photography;
- fun/AOB – horoscopes, quirky interviews, takeaways and recommendations;
- platform extensions – they also have content in podcasts, video content, events, masterclasses and workshops;
- front cover;
- social media assets.

We will now run through the key sections of your own personal branding micro-publication and map out how you comfortably bring your personal brand to life while also aligning with your brand fundamentals.

NEWS

News pages in magazines typically are short and succinct nuggets that grip us and pull us in. They often show imagery and graphics. They quite often have a barometer-style column (e.g. trends going up or down). When we are 'in' our business it can be hard to see what the news nuggets of interest might be. Let's explore how this can work for your audience.

NEWS

Thinking about the year ahead, what news might you have to announce?

- A new product launch?
- A new team recruit?

- A new service offering?
- A new office?
- A new business offering?
- A hybrid way of working half at home/half in the office?
- Perhaps you are collaborating or have a limited edition?
- Any calendar news hooks related to your business?

Note down in the playbook what news items you have coming up. Allow yourself to brainstorm as many as you like and then maybe for our magazine planning sheet just pick the ones that are coming up in the next one to three months.

ACTIVITY 2

PICTURE NEWS

One of the most underrated tools used by small businesses is picture stories. The age-old cliché is that pictures tell us more than words and when crafted well they can really bring the brand personality to life. Whether you actually use your picture to pitch to a national/local news desk it can become a picture in your own micro-publication. Try to make 'behind the scenes picture taking' a habit.

- Do you have any samples or product launches behind the scenes you can share?
- Could you show yourself packing your product or unwrapping your first book, seeing your first article appear online, appearing in print?
- Do you host a lot of workshops or speak at a lot of events?

- Make sure at the very least you are grabbing photos and then you can put them together as a little showreel.

EXAMPLE

PICTURE NEWS

Image of April Fool's day picture story for Yeo Valley who created Moo-R codes on their cows.

Tips

- If you are lost for inspiration download our calendar new hooks PDF from the freebie section of our website, where we give you 35 pages of content ideas.
- The best publicity tip I can give is to read the publications that you want to be featured by and this will help you with the sort of stories that link to your business and your personal brand.

- Share the successes – however humble, however small. Misery loves company, but let's put out what we want to attract.

FEATURES

I define a feature as a trend-led article – usually with a rule of three. Two might be company but three examples show a trend. In my first book, *Hype Yourself,* I talk about how to pitch for these types of features in traditional media. For today, we just want to look at what this looks like and how you can apply it to your business; or at the very least think about some key topic areas that you can own when talking as part of your public relations programme.

In your own notebook or playbook have a think about the following questions and how they could apply to your business.

- *Business*: do you have any interesting HR policies? Do you commute or work in an unusual way? Is the way you recruit unique? What is innovative and unique about how your business operates?
- *Customers:* what is interesting about your audience? Does your business facilitate a consumer behaviour change? Have you had to adapt your offering to meet consumer demand? Are you starting a new trend, and could you put forward two to three other competitors to demonstrate this?
- *Personal:* how has your personal journey shaped your business today? Are there any triumph-over-adversity stories you want to share? Did you have an unusual light bulb moment? Do you run your business with your grandad, twin or is there anything

else unusual about your business set-up? Did you set up the business as a teenager/in your fifties? Check some of the business pages of your national newspaper to get inspired.

- *Data:* what industry reports or category data could you be sharing? Unlike school, it's actually cool now to be the geek of your area. What knowledge bombs can you drop? Do you regularly check the big four or other relevant bigger business reports and use them to hook off for business content?

EXAMPLE

FEATURES

A few examples to get you thinking could be:

- Spill, the remote mental health support for business, decided to pay all their employees the same salary.[17] This in itself tells us that they value people and are looking at solutions to curb the issues around disparity in salary. The programme itself garnered a lot of media attention as well as valuable content and lessons to share across their social channels. In fact, it didn't work and they had to revert to a different salary method, but rather than seeing this as a failure they also used this to share their learnings for the BBC's 'CEO Secrets',[18] which led to one of the biggest drivers of traffic to the website. Sharing the lessons you are learning on the journey makes you relatable and if they go wrong it doesn't show a

---

[17] www.spill.chat/about.
[18] www.bbc.co.uk/news/business-33712313.

vulnerability, it just shows you are human, which all good business should be centred around.

- Rich Leigh, founder of Radioactive PR, used a similar method to garner lots of media and content attention for his public relations business.[19] He set out his stall that they would be trying a four-day work week and along the whole journey shared learnings, including how he was communicating with clients and how they would approach their office absence on the fifth day of the week, which included automating processes and promising clients that if they needed them – just as with an issue or crisis that might happen out of hours – they would be easily contactable. Again, it showed that putting the team first was important to them, as was maintaining good client service, value and communications. It didn't feel like a PR stunt by a PR agency, it felt like a company you then wanted to go and work for.

In each of the aforementioned examples, other companies are included in the feature, and there would be a round-up of arguments for and against the topic, or sometimes an industry analyst or expert commenting on the issue.

Tips

- Remember – stop selling and start sharing. When it comes to sharing your brand's mission, values and purpose, they can all come through from the stories you tell about your company.
- Look outside of your niche. For example, as a PR professional I don't look to place a feature around

---

[19] www.radioactivepr.com.

my business in PR titles because I'm not after industry accolades. My magazine content is for my creative entrepreneur audience and where they are playing.

COMMENT AND OPINION

Magazines and newspapers typically have a section called 'Opinion', which can also be known as guest post or thought leader articles. Writing articles that demonstrate your values, purpose and mission is a great way to bring your brand strategy to life and in the following activity we will look at some easy content pillars to help you do that. I typically group these out into three buckets, and you can go as niche as you want within all of these. A lot of small business owners take for granted the amount of knowledge and expertise that they have. They collect a huge amount of learning, whether that is about the product or service that they offer day in and day out or from their journey to get to this point, then wrap up all the juicy knowledge and pack into a box and pop it under the bed. In this section, we want to think about how we can uncover that box, dust it off and show the brilliance of you that is inside to the world to boost sales, awareness, integrity and SEO for your business.

ACTIVITY

COMMENT AND OPINION – CREATE YOUR OWN CONTENT

This is about generating ideas for content that you could create. Have a look at each of the categories and try to note down two or three ideas for each.

Expertise: Think about the topics that you get asked about the most – or maybe the things you wish you were asked about! Maybe you have some insight on the biggest problems or challenges you see your customers have in this space. Here are some prompts that will help you generate ideas in the expertise category.

- Top five tips to...
- How to XX by doing YY
- What I learnt from XX
- Three time-saving hacks to...
- One must-have trick to...
- The success of your team
- Industry trends
- Unique methodologies you use
- Expertise.

A lot of my expertise content revolves around publicity tips, creating a media kit, pitching to journalists, showing how to elevate your personal brand. I often create expertise content based around current client work or questions that I am asked on a regular basis.

Human interest: Many business founders have set up their company for a personal reason; it could be they spotted a gap in the market, maybe they had a poor experience of working in-house for another company, perhaps they were not able to keep up the traditional way of working that they had previously.

Under the human-interest pillar, jot down any personal stories that you feel comfortable talking about that relate to your business. You don't have to share anything you don't feel comfortable with, but don't worry about sharing a failure or a negative experience – it doesn't make you look bad; it makes you relatable and likeable.

Think about what other people could learn from the experience.

HUMAN INTEREST

Derrick Grant, founder of www.thinkwillow.com and www. guidesticks.com, created his death-tech businesses to solve the problems he faced when supporting a friend through a funeral. While the businesses are both part of the emerging death-tech category, which has seen an increase in start-ups and funding in this space, his reason for creating these businesses makes him relatable and we can emotionally connect with his story.

Passion points: What do you do as a hobby or as a personal interest that you can relate to your business? What inspires your work? What cultural movements and moments inspire your business? How do you apply any behaviour traits associated with your hobbies to your day job? Or is your hobby your day job?

PASSION POINTS

I saw photographer Adam Brazier talk about the similarities between learning to grow tomato plants in lockdown and growing a social media following. But what was really engaging was that he included a photo of his tomato plants. It gave us a sense of what he does in his spare time and a glimpse into his personal life, without it being too revealing.

He also made really succinct points, meaning that his post was relatable whether you were a novice or advanced at social media growth strategies.

Tips

- Consider creating a content calendar or schedule of articles that you promote on platforms such as The Dots or LinkedIn to showcase your expertise.
- If you are more of a natural talker than a writer, record your article on a transcription tool like Trint or Otter.ai.
- If you are completely clueless around what topics you might start with, try askmeanything.com or quora.com and insert the keyword that relates to your business to get an idea of what questions people are asking about it.
- Try to keep adding to the notes on your phone or a notebook of strong opinions you have about your world, or regular questions that you are asked.
- Try a platform like LinkedIn or Medium to start getting your industry expertise out there.

PERSONAL BRANDING PHOTOGRAPHY

In Chapter 2 we talked about imagery. If you haven't read that chapter yet (you rebel you!), it will give you a basic insight into the wider use of correct framing and layout to make the most of your brand. In this section, we're looking more specifically at the importance of using photography in your personal branding. For four years, I had a faceless business – no one knew what I looked like or who I was. Since making the strategic pivot of putting myself out there as an industry expert, I have been able to foster new revenue streams in addition to those developed from the purely business side.

Even if you don't want to be the face of your brand on social media channels I would say if you ever think you want to gain publicity for the business then you 100% need them.

Headshots

To be able to use yourself as a tool to amplify your business you need to get some decent headshots! If you get booked for a conference, a podcast, a social media takeover, featured in a national newspaper, etc., then it is more than likely that one of the first things you will be asked for is a photo of yourself. When it comes to a personal branding photographer, I would be inclined to pick someone whose work you admire, rather than just looking for the cheapest. If you can't afford to pay a professional photographer's rates, can you offer a skill swap instead?

Depending on the photographer you work with, they may very well have their own briefing template, which will make it easier for you to tell them what you want. If they don't, though, there's nothing stopping you from creating your own! Here's a quick template you could use:

Photography briefing template	
Proposed date of shoot	
Where will images be used?	*E.g. social media, press shots, marketing materials, etc.*
Ideal shots required	
Key brand colours or themes	*Use the work you did in Chapter 1!*

Brand values	*Use the work you did in Chapter 1!*
Suggested prop list	

We spoke with sales and visibility expert Sara Dalrymple to gather some of her top personal branding photography tips:

1. *Create genuine laughter and smiles.* It's worth thinking in advance of the session how you want people to experience you for the first time. What are the values that you've built your business on? How can you show your potential clients what it'll be like working with you through the photos you create? This is important because your headshot is the first chance your clients get to see and connect with you, the person behind the brand. In order for clients you haven't even met yet to want to pick up the phone and work with you, your smiley headshot does so much work for you in terms of giving off warmth and approachability and showing what a good egg you are! These smiles need to be genuine, rather than staged, so it's crucial to work with a photographer who you get on really well with and can have a laugh with. If you feel happy around your photographer, your warmth will shine through effortlessly. Absolutely no stuffy, staged or awkward posing allowed!

2. *Pick personally.* Get the right photographer for YOU! Before you start looking for a photographer, have a think about how you are in front of a camera and the kinds of photos you want to capture. For example, if you know you feel shy and awkward around a camera, it's definitely worth making sure you find someone who specializes in putting people

at ease. When it comes to style, every photographer has their own individual way of shooting, so it's important to find out whether what they specialize in matches what you're looking for. Obviously, you need to love their style and the photos they capture, but it's also really important that your photographer is someone you could and would be friends with.

3. *Mix it up.* Ensure you have a mixture of photos of you looking at the camera and more candid shots. Eye contact is key when it comes to fostering connection and building trust, but your clients also want to see you in action, whether that's at work, walking in your local area or just having a coffee. It all helps to tell the story of your brand! Search Pinterest for inspiration – 15 pins or so will give you the opportunity to notice the poses, backdrops and style you favour most. Make sure to grab plenty of well-framed landscape shots too – they're essential for media and websites.

4. *Align your photos to your brand.* If you're a bright and colourful person, for example, make sure your headshots aren't taken in a neutral colour palette. Your photos are there to represent you and your brand until you can do so in person, so show up for your photo shoot wearing pops of colour in your brand colours and an outfit that you might wear if you were meeting clients, as these details all help build strong brand identity and give an overall impression of professionalism and consistency. Wear something you feel comfortable but amazing in, as the number one aim for your photo session is for you to look like YOU. For some people this might mean trainers and a denim jacket, for others, a smart dress and jacket – the key is to keep it real. This is equally true when it comes to pairing up your photos to your copy. If your website is written in one style, and your photos are

taken in completely another, it's going to be jarring for your clients. One of the key roles of your brand photography is to bring the copy on your website to life, so it needs to marry up to your messaging and be cohesive in terms of the overall impression you're giving.

5. *Relax.* Having your headshots taken should NOT make you feel nervous: it's for the photographer to work out how to get the best out of you and find the right light, etc., so turn up with your shoulders back and your head held high and don't worry about a thing!

ACTIVITY

PERSONAL BRANDING PHOTOGRAPHY MOOD BOARD

We created a mood board for your business in Chapter 2 – if you were keen, maybe you created a few for specific uses! Now it's time to create one for your personal brand photography. Just as before, use a tool like Pinterest, PowerPoint or a physical board if you like to get hands-on, and start searching for images that you like. Consider using headshots of fellow founders – but you can also use any well-constructed shots that you like. Remember: make sure the images match your brand values!

- Collate images of headshots you like by searching the social media sites mentioned above or from magazines.
- As you start to group them together, are there any particular themes, colours or styles that stick out to you?

- Reflect on your brand values and search for images that you feel embody these words.
- If there is a particular magazine or publication that you want to be featured in, look at the headshots they use. Cut them out and put them in your workbook/playbook or drag and drop into your digital mood board.
- Remind yourself of your brand values and add them to the worksheet so that when you show your photographer they can understand exactly what you're aiming for.

EXAMPLE

PERSONAL BRANDING PHOTOGRAPHY MOOD BOARD

I worked with photographer Almass Badatt on creating a mood board of shots and a style I was hoping for before we created my first personal branding photos.

HACK

Think about the framing of the shots. If nothing else, for marketing materials you need a straight headshot, with your head and shoulders facing the camera and you looking straight on.

EXAMPLE

HEADSHOT CONSTRUCTION

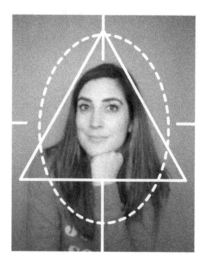

Tips

– It is always worth looking at your competitors' photography, but don't replicate it – that would defeat the purpose.

- How can you bring your own signature brand into your lifestyle shots? Think about the clothes you wear and the products you are holding to enforce your brand values.
- Can you make the space feel on brand? At the very least it needs to be clear so that you can easily cut it out and *make* it on brand.
- Always, ALWAYS get a landscape version of each shot; it's a great tool for helping to make more of a land grab if featured in traditional media and most websites are framed in landscape so it's automatically going to be better framed for you.
- Make sure you get a few variations of the signature headshot with different clothes/backgrounds so that you have different options to use and different styles for different formats.

FUN/AOB

How can you add a bit of extra sauce to your magazine? What is uniquely different about you that you might want to share? Again this isn't about getting your face in front of the camera all day long, but what feels comfortable that you could share that shows a bit about you and links to your workplace?

Most business owners have something that they do to relax or wind down, and the more unique the better. Hadrien and I often share places we have visited, music, shows we are watching on Netflix or activities we get up to. One of the things we love about London and the small business community is discovering all the cool and quirky things there are to do. We demonstrate our support for championing small businesses by trying to showcase not just the people we work with but other discoveries we make.

Some of my most engaged posts were talking about the Netflix show *Tiger King* or the Fyre Festival (with my own publicity spin of course), and our most liked post to date was when I took part in the #gettymuseumchallenge during the first pandemic lockdown of 2020 and dressed up as a famous artwork!

FUN/AOB

In your notebook or playbook note down the following:

- What do you do outside of your day job that gets you inspired?
- What are your hobbies?
- What makes you unique?

If you are struggling, think about the lifestyle sections of a newspaper or magazine. Which parts do you gravitate towards? Reality TV gossip? Fashion? Astrology?

Thinking about these wider lifestyle areas of interest, how can you bring these into the public domain?

Note: For the more camera-shy folks, this is a great opportunity to share who you are and what you're about without being the actual face of the brand.

FUN/AOB

One of my good business friends and a great example of someone who has nailed the personal brand without revealing their private life is Kim Darragon, founder of Kim Does Marketing. We asked her to share one of her top tips around personal branding:

Don't be vanilla – be interesting! If you're guava, be guava! Own it and spread the word about it. Don't overshare the same tired trends and memes that everyone else does, particularly if you haven't yet clearly defined who you are and your brand personality on digital platforms. Jumping on the viral mainstream wagon might give you some exposure in the short run, but it will lose its effectiveness in the long run if you haven't defined your tone of voice. In a sea of social media sameness, trends fade but personality stays. Focus on yourself, watch the competition (but not too closely!) and honestly define what makes you unique.

You don't need to meet Kim to know that she is a marketing expert who does her homework by sharing lots of research, tips and tricks. But she also refers to her South East Asian and French cultural roots as well as her love for ice cream, fashion, small biz and reading. You can get a sense of who she is without her doing talking stories.

Tips

- Work is just one component of who we are, but don't be shy about sharing more than this.

- I often use popular TV shows from Netflix that I've been watching and put a PR spin on them to showcase my expertise but tap into the cultural zeitgeist.
- Nothing is too niche – if you are an embroidery expert with a penchant for *Murder She Wrote* so be it…

PERSONAL BRAND IN THE WILD

When print publications started out these were the only touchpoints, but now most successful digital media outlets have several digital touchpoints to reach their audience and make the most of their assets. In this section, I want to get you thinking about the different ways you could be bringing your own micro-publication to life in the way that best suits your own personality.

This is not about being everywhere but rather being in the place that resonates with your target audience. It's also an opportunity to take strides away from your competitive set. In the following activity section we list a few ways that you could be amplifying your personal brand from the work we have done in the previous chapters.

ACTIVITY

PERSONAL BRAND IN THE WILD

You may already be doing one or none of these activities, but they are an opportunity for you to audit and reflect on how you already use them and how you could amplify your brand within these, moving forward.

I'd also encourage you to revisit the content ideas you created earlier in the chapter in the news, features and comment and opinion sections, to see how else you can bring your magazine content to life and see if you can find new opportunities to elevate your profile, reach a bigger audience and provide greater opportunities for your business.

Guest talks/workshops

- Where and how are you bringing your brand to life in speaking opportunities?
- Are you creating presentations or materials that are representative of your brand look and feel?
- Who are you doing the talk/workshop for? If someone else, how does their company align with your brand values? Do they have a diverse and inclusive speaker roster?
- If you are a jeans and trainers person, is this the sort of event where you are supposed to wear a suit? If so, is this really the best brand fit for your business/audience?

Pros and cons: great for people who enjoy face-to-face connections. A brilliant way to take your expertise from one to many. May take time to pitch and secure and often require development time to prepare interactive and engaging content.

Brochures/PDFs/downloadable templates

- Do you have a consistent brand look and feel in your collateral materials?
- Do you need to create a set of templates for your business requirements?

- Are you including a copyright note in your downloads?

Pros and cons: brilliant for natural writers. Need regular reviewing to ensure they are kept up to date. Once created can be widely distributed and shared. May work very well as a lead magnet to attract a new audience.

Newsletter

- Arguably the newsletter is the most powerful tool for engaging your audience (although that is a different book entirely). How is your newsletter looking?
- What is the editorial style of your newsletter? Do you need to provide guidelines for it to be outsourced?
- What images and photos are you using? How is your brand being used through this touchpoint?

Pros and cons: social media posts are often only organically seen by just 4% of your audience but a healthy newsletter open rate can hit many more than this. It is a great sales tool and a way to connect with your audience and keep the customers warm from data that you actually own (rather than being in the hands of a social media company).

Podcasts

- Are you proactively asking to appear on other people's podcasts, or do you regularly put out content on your own?
- When sharing podcast episodes, are you using an audiogram tool or using your own brand to share the episode?
- How can you expand your audience and cement your brand persona by being selective about the podcasts you appear on?

Pros and cons: if you are time poor, it may be easier to focus on being a guest on other people's podcasts rather than your own as they will have a ready-made audience and are in control of most of the marketing.

SOCIAL MEDIA

At the time of writing, the big eight are Clubhouse, Facebook, LinkedIn, Twitter, Instagram, YouTube, TikTok and Pinterest. Personally, because I work in the creative entrepreneur space, I also have a huge amount of time for The Dots, which is like LinkedIn for non-suit wearers. There may be other platforms that are relevant to your niche; the key is to know where your audience will be looking for you and to apply the following activity to those spaces.

ACTIVITY

SOCIAL MEDIA

Make sure you do a quarterly review of your social media feeds and check that you have a clear personal brand thread running across them.

- Have you covered all the business basics? Such as contact details or preferred method of contact (e.g. direct messages (DMs) or phone)?
- Social media banners: you need to make sure that you have a call to action on social media banners. When people are clicking on your profile they are more often than not looking at the images rather than the information. There is an opportunity here to direct your audience to what you want them to do.

Is it subscribe to your newsletter? Notice a special offer? Book a freebie? Download a template?

- Bio: are you giving a succinct one-liner on what you do? All too often we try to tell people everything about us, but think about your headline. I'm a PR expert, for example. What I do is so much more than that but this bio summary is the Ronseal 'Does what it says on the tin'!
- Image: a clear, face-on headshot in proportion, head and shoulders, as we described in the headshot section above. You don't want a photo of you on your holidays in your sunglasses.
- Logo: remember what we said about logos, about not necessarily fitting the whole brand name in. Have a clear and consistent avatar across all your social media channels.

Tips

- Getting your branding correct across all the social media channels can be a mammoth task. In your magazine plan, write the key touchpoints you need to prioritize and put a timeline together for tidying them up.
- Make sure you have a quarterly spring clean – does your headshot/bio need to be updated or any other tweaks made to reflect who you are/where your business is currently at?
- Do you have a personal feed or a brand feed? It may be the case that you have a brand feed but use your headshot on it if you are a solopreneur to make people connect. When you are starting out, it is hard work to make more than one feed, so streamline where you can.

- Consider a company billboard feed on all channels – where you direct people to your other accounts that you proactively use.
- Use namecheckr.com to get your handle.

HOW TO GET PERSONAL BRANDING RIGHT

The biggest challenge for a lot of business owners is to get the personal branding balance right. They are worried about sharing too much or having to have too much of an online presence. So let's just delve a little bit into how we can be mindful.

It is confusing to your audience if you are changing your name or your colours regularly. While there is absolutely room for a brand refresh or evolution, you don't want to undo the brand legacy you have built. While this whole chapter focuses on your personal brand, I would like to stress that it should be and feel natural. It's not a made-up persona, it's about being unequivocally who you are but choosing how much of yourself you want to share as an extension of your business and in a way that works for you.

Many people get caught up by worrying about what they share online, but what you need to remember is that your social channels and what you are sharing for your personal brand is like the version of yourself you would bring to the office. Almost all of us have got practice doing this – it's just about shifting that online! Nevertheless, here are a few things to think about, to help with any social media anxiety.

1. Share any big business news with your close friends or family before you announce online. They might

not be thrilled to find out these things in such a non-personal way.

2. If you are feeling emotional about a situation in business, don't post for at least twenty-four hours – give yourself space to process first.

3. If you are under attack on your socials, don't feel rushed to share a response. Just like dealing with a customer email complaint, let them know you are looking at the situation and that you will respond in due course.

4. Be mindful of who you are following and liking. Hitting a 'like' button is a public endorsement for that person and their business practices. If you wouldn't publicly collaborate with this business or person, then don't go keen on the 'like' button either.

5. Support your friends in the community. If someone has had their work copied, been asked to speak for free at an event when others are being paid, been bullied or taken advantage of by someone in your network, then stop following the perpetrator. We have a duty as small business owners to support and promote those in our community. When small businesses are complicit in bad behaviour, it's not only unethical but it can also affect their personal brand.

6. Whatever you share on social media is a digital thumbprint. Don't let a second in time come back to bite you later!

And a final note: while I would always love you to show who is the face behind the business (and it certainly helps with the storytelling part of a public relations campaign), you absolutely can bring the personality of the founders through without talking on camera. Extreme yet successful examples of anonymity could be Daft Punk, Sia or Banksy.

Tips

- If you wouldn't say it to a colleague at some work drinks, then don't say it on social media.
- Has a comment made you feel emotional? If so, wait before you react.
- It doesn't matter that some people won't like you, they are not your people. There will be people that love you too – don't focus on the naysayers.
- As a final check before you share something, ask yourself: does this add value?

CHAPTER SUMMARY

Chapter 3 has been about condensing all the work we have done so far and thinking of our personal brand like a magazine. By thinking of yourself as a micro-publication you can look at your content pillars and map out balanced content to connect with your audience.

At the end of this chapter you should have an understanding of the following:

- What a personal brand is and why it's important.
- Where your personal brand is right now.
- How to plan out some news, feature, comment and opinion segments.
- Personal branding photography, why you need it and how to secure the best imagery.

- Ways we can bring our new magazine edit of a personal brand to life on social media.
- A few warnings on some watch-outs.

In the next chapter, you'll get thinking about all of the fun and creative ways you could use your business brand to help amplify and project your brand personality.

CHAPTER 4

LOW BUDGET FOR BIG IMPACT

QUOTE

BE SURPRISING. CREATE FANS.

Hadrien Châtelet

In this chapter, we wanted to spark some ideas. We know that small business owners can sometimes be restricted by budget, time and confidence, so we wanted to share some examples to get you juiced.

Remember that, essentially, all good brands and publicity make you *feel something*. Creating something standout that evokes humour, shareability or sparks conversation is a simple trick to help you raise more awareness. While there is not necessarily a measurable return on investment for this, think of it as micro-billboards for your business. Even better, some of these tools already play into what you might need in your toolkit, and with a small twist can emphasize your service or product.

MAXIMIZING YOUR BRAND

We are going to give a brief description of a few examples under the following categories:

- *office branding*: a few examples of how to create a lasting impression;
- *business cards*: don't have to be a dry tool that ends up in the bin;
- *prompt cards*: bring your expertise to tangible life;
- *brand collaboration*: create talkability and share audiences;
- *eco/sustainable design*: make a product with purpose;
- *accessible design*: packaging for visually impaired people;
- *surprise and delight*: give your audience some surprise and delight moments;
- *brand merch*: products, clothes and accessories;

- *quirky uses*: a few other random ideas to spark yours;
- *best of the rest*: a few brand considerations when building your social channels.

OFFICE BRANDING

We live in a visual world. While you might not have the budget of a Silicon Valley tech start-up, there are ways we can bring our brand into our office space to create a lasting impression.

EXAMPLE 1

LEONA BAKER

Leona Baker, otherwise known as Indie Roller, is a great example of a business with a fab office interior. Leona champions indie business owners in a multitude of ways, and used to have her own subscription business called Lucky Dip Club. From the giant pink, yellow, blue and white rays of a sunshine scene on her wall, to the multiple indie brands she shows support to by using their products in her space, she often likens her surroundings to visual encouragement to get her through the day. It's memorable, it's photogenic and it completely embodies her brand.

EXAMPLE 2

EAST OF EDEN

It doesn't all need to be wild colours or paraphernalia. For example, we worked with yoga studio East of Eden in Walthamstow to create a brand and colour palette that brought the feeling of an urban Eden, this inclusive community, to life. Not only is this branding used in their social media assets, but the studio space itself has the brand woven throughout. From the geometric shapes seen on their Instagram and website that appear on the walls and in the glass bricks and tiling patterns, through to the colours in their interior design paint palette.

EXAMPLE 3

THE WERN

When we created our own home office, our builder Rich from Arc Creations took one look at us and said, 'I don't think you are white shelf kinda people' – and he is right. As he followed our Instagram accounts, he suggested weaving in brand elements into the final fit-out. This included using our brand colours on our office shelves to create a rainbow effect, and using the signature green in the skirting and around the door frame to give a pop of colour. Without fail, the first time anyone meets us online or visits the space they feel our brand values and personality come through – and we receive a lot of compliments!

Tips

 – Can you use your office branding to help secure press coverage? A landscape image of us helped secure us the lead image in a 'working from home' article in London's *Evening Standard*. Have a Google of 'Hadrien Châtelet' and 'working from home' to see the article.

- If your background matches your brand palette for social media it can be a really easy way for you to film content or take photos that easily fit into your feeds. BUT don't worry if it doesn't; think about using a cover image instead – can you bring elements of your brand to life with a few simple props or wall art?

BUSINESS CARDS

The simple business card has been a subject of much debate. Personally, I've used a unique, coloured business card printed on G. F. Smith paper that has been extremely useful at events, conferences and workshops, allowing people we meet to be able to follow up with either me or Hadrien. If business cards are something that you think will be useful for you and your brand, here are three different examples of business cards done well that I think not only enhance the business's brand proposition but help them stick in your mind.

EXAMPLE 1

JEAN JULLIEN - THE CREATIVE HANDSHAKE

Jean Jullien took the concept of the business card to its more primary function; a business card is a greeting, a handshake (well it was before we did elbow taps), it's a way to introduce yourself. For this reason, Jean simply designed a business card in the form of a hand, where the fingers can be folded to convey different attitudes and messages. To be even more effective, he produced not only one card but developed the service to use different shades of skin colour. Jean made the cards in collaboration with Jukebox Print.[20]

EXAMPLE 2

PRIVACY MATTERS – OVERLAY OF INK FOR GDPR

In May 2019, new data protection laws came into effect in the UK. Around that time, I don't think we could take a breath on social media without a mention of general data protection regulation (GDPR)! Graphic designer Hugo Araujo from Studio HAGA designed the identity of Privacy Matters, a consultancy company that works in GDPR and digital data protection. They thought that a good way to transmit the purpose and mission of the company on the first impression was to protect its own data in the business cards. So as a creative spin, they created a layer of special, scratchable ink on the cards, hiding and protecting the contact information initially and revealing it only to the client that needs to access the data.

EXAMPLE 3

LUSH – LAWN SEEDS FOR A LAWN AND PROPERTY ENHANCEMENT COMPANY

Creative agency Struck developed a business card that is also a mini packet of lawn seeds. The US-based lawn and

---

20 www.jukeboxprint.com/jean-jullien-business-cards.

property enhancement company Lush had their company details and contact information on the front, and instructions for seed planting with a call to action to use them on the back. It complements the company mission.

Tips

- There are countless articles out there highlighting great business cards. Have a Google of 'creative uses of business cards' and see what you get inspired by.
- Can you include business card information in other brand assets that you might use (e.g. compliments slips, gift cards or notepads)?

PROMPT CARDS

In the digital era, it's actually really refreshing sometimes to have printed materials and prompts to get us thinking. More often than not, unlike a book that you might read and then put down, prompt cards remind us to take action and are a great way for your target audience to live your ethos.

EXAMPLE 1

FREEDOM & BALANCE – SCHOOL IN YOUR POCKET

Freedom & Balance is an art college for the artist in everyone. Andre describes his prompt cards as the equivalent of his school in his pocket. It means wherever he goes, he can instantly bring his teaching and exercises to life by pulling a card out of the box. He has turned his syllabus into 56 creative exercises for everyone. Each card uses his teachings to help explore what his version of a creative industry could look like, how to build it and what it could offer to the world.

EXAMPLE 2

THE WERN – 52 PR TIPS

We had a dual motive for creating our own pack of 52 PR tips. First, Hadrien had joined the business and we wanted to showcase the branding side. A tangible product was a great way to bring his work to life. Second, I found that when people would come to talks or workshops, or read my book, there was only so much information that they could retain. The prompt cards give handy reminders and help keep small business owners accountable to themselves with short PR prompts. We sell the PR tips either individually or with my book *Hype Yourself* as a PR starter kit.

EXAMPLE 3

GET LIT RETREATS – THE GET LIT CARDS

Aisha Carrington, founder of the Get Lit retreats, used products to help pivot her business and broaden her services. Today she facilitates meditations, sound baths and is a spiritual guide. Her Get Lit cards are a tangible embodiment of her brand. Each card comes with an affirmation and meditations to help you with your self-love journey, and a song recommendation. Music and dancing are key signature components of Aisha's retreats.

BRAND COLLABORATION

Brand collaborations or partnerships are a great way for small businesses to raise their profile, build their audience and cement their positioning in the market – especially when you are just starting out, or when you find yourself in a bit of a business rut. Rather than thinking about how you can make your next sale, you want to be thinking about who you could be partnering with to raise awareness of your brand.

EXAMPLE 1

KANKAN X SUPERMUNDANE

Graphic designer and artist Supermundane created a limited edition super soap design, wrapping paper and gift card for eco-friendly soap in a can superstars KANKAN for Christmas. What was particularly ingenious, is that anyone who purchased this seasonal bundle were gifted a set of gift cards he had created with the brand name subtly stamped on the back – meaning that more festive cheer could be passed on and even more brand awareness.

EXAMPLE 2

ZARA CERAMICS

Zara successfully grew her business in lockdown in a series of collaborations that were vital tools for progression, so we invited her to share a few thoughts:

The first big collaboration was with another local business, Ted & Stitch, who embroider jumpers. Unlikely pairing but we put together a jumper and mug combination and promoted it heavily on both of our platforms. The benefit of this meant that we were both experiencing exposure from each other's platforms opening us up to new customers. And that it gave me someone else to work with. When you are self-employed it can get very lonely and for me, I find it quite boring being home on my own all day when I was used to being in a studio filled with other creatives while I was at uni.

Another advantage for me when collaborating with a candle maker (Olivia's Haven), where she made the wax melts and I made the wax burners, was that it allowed me to experiment with a new product and gave me an audience to sell the product to that I may not have already been exposed to. When I collaborated with Olivia's Haven she already had an audience who were interested in candles, so I was able to tap into that market as well as also offering my customers up to her and we both bounced off each other really well.

Collaborating taught me what kind of products sell well in my industry and also what doesn't sell as well. It also taught me how to work with other people. Because of my niche being a potter, it's not common for you to work with other people so this gave me an outlet and an opportunity to network to a much larger scale, which is something I couldn't have done had I only made and sold my own.

EXAMPLE 3

SIMBA AND SLOANE

For their first product Simba and Sloane wanted to create something that celebrated the iconic attributes of black British musicians. Creating a literal representation was never going to be the aim, so they sought out an illustrator with an abstract and suggestive style to collaborate with – thus creating the perfect partnership. By chance they stumbled across Chidiabii Studio. The illustrations needed to point towards iconic attributes of the artist, without revealing them. They wanted to create curiosity and conversation as well as a unique item and Adryan's reductive style leant itself to this aspect of the brief. They also wanted to ensure there was gender parity. A normal card pack has four jacks, so they decided to replace these with two princes and princesses. The card deck illustrations were finally coupled with Simba and Sloane's brand typeface to create a memorable artefact for the company.

Tips

Some things to consider before making a collaboration:

- Have I done due diligence on the brand, service person, etc.?
- Are both potential partners bringing something to the table? It shouldn't just be one person benefitting from the partnership.
- Have you agreed a cross-promotion? Are you both doing the legwork?

ECO/SUSTAINABLE DESIGN

There have been extensive reports that focus on the increase in consumers seeking brands with purpose.[21] With climate change a hot topic, an important brand consideration is whether you can underpin your business with a bigger purpose in terms of eco and sustainable credentials.

EXAMPLE 1

MORE THAN SWIM

A sustainable swimwear company all handmade to order in the UK, whose tagline is: 'Minimizing your carbon footprint, maximizing your sass!' Founder Sandra has created bespoke hand-illustrated designs inspired by endangered species that you can't find anywhere else. All packaging is eco-friendly, recyclable, FSC certified and UK sourced. As well as being mindful of the visual element and evoking a joyful, happy (eco-conscious) feeling by using bright colours that harmonize beautifully together, the swimsuits are delivered to your door in a gorgeous, recycled box with branding (recycled stickers and tags), a branded drawstring eco-cotton reusable bag and protective recyclable outer packaging. Head to https://morethanswim.com to get inspired.

---

[21] See www2.deloitte.com/content/dam/insights/us/articles/6963_ global-marketing-trends/DI_2021-Global-Marketing-Trends_ Purpose_US.pdf.

EXAMPLE 2

KANKAN

Another mention for small business brand KANKAN who are smashing their eco and sustainable credentials. The product itself is cruelty-free and made with natural ingredients and essential oils. It is served in an infinitely recyclable can, so that you can easily refill the glass dispenser. One tree is planted for every can sold. If you buy a gift set, it also arrives in a recyclable cardboard overlay. Visit www.kankan.london for more information.

EXAMPLE 3

OVER ALL 1516

Ethical clothing brand Over All 1516 is creating sustainable packaging for sending out their product that has multiple uses. Founder Eirlie will be custom-printing pizza boxes – a nod to the pizza she lived off in the early days of Over All, when it was the only takeaway she could get that met her family's allergy requirements. Pizza picnics, which consisted of eating pizza on a blanket on the living room floor, became a mini tradition when juggling single parenting and work deadlines. On the insides of the boxes Eirlie has created activities for kids (and adults), printed so that not only is it a nice unboxing experience, but you get multiple uses out of it. Everything will be recyclable, including the printed packing tape and thank-you notes, which are made in-house from recycled pattern card offcuts.

ACCESSIBLE DESIGN FOR BLIND AND VISUALLY IMPAIRED CONSUMERS

The World Health Organization states that globally the number of visually impaired people of all ages is estimated to be 285 million, of whom 39 million are registered as blind.[22] The first go-to as a solution for accessible packaging for visually impaired people is to use Braille.[23] Under EU Law this is a requirement for all medical packaging, but there is no such obligation for consumer packaging. However, according to the National Federation of the Blind (NFB), fewer than 10% of registered blind people in the United States can read Braille and only 10% of blind children are learning it. So how can we incorporate packaging design into our business?

Sadly, while looking for case studies for this book I struggled to find many examples of small businesses with accessible design for visually impaired people, so I did have to lean on a few bigger businesses for examples. Hopefully, as these options become more mainstream, there will be more opportunities for small businesses to implement them and the costs will be lower.

EXAMPLE 1

MIMICA

Voguebusiness.com reported on food-tech start-up Mimica, who created tactile labels that use biodegradable gel. They

---

[22] www.who.int/blindness/publications/globaldata/en/.

[23] https://inside-packaging.nridigital.com/packaging_jul20/accessible_packaging_visually_impaired.

are smooth to touch when food is fresh but go bumpy once the ingredients pass their expiry date. This has a dual function as not only does it tell the consumer when their product is past its expiry date, but it is also something that sighted customers can use.[24]

The same *Vogue Business* article cites intuitive designs like open-and-close caps and magnetic closures trending among package makers, according to Mordor Intelligence, with many customers finding the audial assurance satisfactory. It isn't just about designing packaging that is easier to read but also about considering how to open and use it.

EXAMPLE 2

PROCTER & GAMBLE

The use of symbols rather than Braille is also increasing in popularity. At a global level Procter & Gamble have led the charge using Herbal Essences' bottles featuring tactile marks that allow people to identify them by touch. It includes stripes on shampoo and circles on conditioners. The benefit of shapes in design make it accessible for all and means you don't need to learn Braille. It's also great for glasses or contact lens wearers who might usually have blurry vision in the shower.

---

[24] www.voguebusiness.com/beauty/braille-beauty-packaging-loccitane.

SURPRISE AND DELIGHT

I'm going to make the assumption that if you have got this far in the book, you are a small business owner who not only wants to learn how to build your brand but are also interested in a bigger mission than just making money for yourself. One of the most important ways you build your brand is by how you make your existing audience *feel*. We asked customer service expert Misch Fretwell from Chatterbox Consulting to share with us some thoughts to get us pumped up about giving some surprise and delight moments to our audience:

Think of your customers like you do the people you care about. Your business earns the right to sell to customers through the trust you build. If you ignore them to move on to the next shiny thing? They're likely to get what they need elsewhere.

One happy customer will sing your praises but the unhappy ones will tell double or triple the people to avoid your business and most of them will probably never tell you. So, get to know what makes your customers tick. Surprise them, excite them, listen to their problems. Give them no option but to come back and tell their peers about how well you looked after them. It's five times cheaper than ploughing time and money into the abyss of a cold audience and it could boost your profits up to 95%.

EXAMPLE 1

MAILCHIMP

As a Mailchimp partner we recently received an unprompted partner gift. Inside was a selection of useful and functional gifts, each of which has been created with other Mailchimp partners' products and co-branded. We already felt great about them – but this just solidified our experience! Mailchimp feel aligned with our brand values because they are all about championing the underdog; to us, even though they are a big global entity, they have the small business feel to them.

EXAMPLE 2

KEY PERSON OF INFLUENCE PROGRAMME

As part of the membership to the 40-week Key Person of Influence (KPI) business accelerator programme, every cohort member received a syllabus and gift package in the post. Within the box, there were multiple personalized goods including fortune cookies, mugs and printed materials from the course with a ring binder to file away your top thinking. There were also several copies of the book the course was based on so that you could pass on copies to your contacts and, of course, become advocates and spread word of the business.[25]

---

[25] See www.keypersonofinfluence.com/kpi-method/.

EXAMPLE 3

SEO BUNDLE

Menekse Stewart runs a very popular SEO programme called the SEO Bundle, which teaches small businesses how to master SEO without needing to pay expensive agency fees. Graphic designer Liz Mosley developed a rebrand for the course and gave all the course materials a really fun and vibrant look to try and counteract what many perceive to be the dull and serious nature of SEO. Menekse wanted to create a playful and creative box of goodies to send out to all new students. The box included a personalized branded bar of Tony's Chocolonely chocolate with an entertaining slogan on the front. It was a lovely way to surprise and delight students and bring some humour to a traditionally serious topic.

Tips

- We can often be focused on the next customer rather than looking at how can we give back more to our current audience. When was the last time you thought about what extra value you could give?
- Surprise and delight moments don't have to be tangible gifts. They could be a useful e-book, video or blog post that will help solve customers' problems.

BRAND MERCH

We touched on a few business gifts in the surprise and delight section but if there's one thing that is important to remember about business merch or goodies, it's that you don't want to create items for the sake of it. Make sure whatever you are making to give away has a specific and planned purpose. Nobody wants a branded pen, USB stick or mouse mat anymore; and if I'm honest, I've probably been sent rather a lot of branded mugs in the last year too. Here are a few examples of brands who create merch that fits with their brand.

EXAMPLE 1

DUCKIE

They Them Studio have created some exciting branded tins and records for Duckie, a really creative organization that started producing club nights 25 years ago, originally with a DIY aesthetic. This is something that They Them Studio still include today as part of their brand. They have a solid history of changing everyday objects to make Duckie collectibles instead of paper flyers for some of their events. The records are bought as a job lot from eBay. The tin cans are baked beans with labels stuck over the top; these advertised a food-based show about Fanny Craddock at Walthamstow Assembly Hall. Anything can be turned into an advert; stickers are your friend.

EXAMPLE 2

SPILL

Why on earth did Spill, a therapy start-up, make the world's most ridiculous fashion video? Because when they surveyed their users about what stopped them from accessing therapy before, they often heard quotes like: 'Therapy can seem really daunting – I was worried about taking the plunge.' Part of the way they're trying to disrupt this 'intimidating and serious' stereotype is with their Slack app, which aims to make it easier for anyone to start therapy. But they also want to create a bigger movement, one that repositions therapy as totally normal – and even (gasp) fun! That's why they launched a collection of loud-and-proud pro-therapy merchandise and why they did potentially the most ridiculous fashion shoot ever to promote it. Sometimes the way you make serious changes in the world is by not taking yourself too seriously.

EXAMPLE 3

THE SELFHOOD X MIND

The Selfhood partnered with two local Mind charities on a fundraising campaign called #checkyourselfbefore yournotifications. As The Selfhood focuses on social media tips and tricks it was a great fit. Daisy, the founder, is also keen to remind us not to get too sucked into the social media bubble, so the charity cause is fully aligned with what she does as a brand.

QUIRKY USES OF BRANDS BROUGHT TO LIFE

Here we just wanted to give a few nods to some of our other favourites we have seen in our daily life or been told about by our network. The list is endless but here are our final three. Make sure you give us a tag on socials if you ever spy great ones in the wild – @hadrienchâtelet in particular loves to give a voice to great uses of brand.

OTHER SCENTS

They Them Studio worked with Other Scents, a perfume brand for all genders, where they printed the cards on to uncoated paper, then used an affordable perforator, and made a rip line along the card where the colour meets white. This can then be torn off and used to spray and waft the perfume.

THRIVA.CO

When we traditionally think of medical testing kits we don't necessarily think about cool brand and packaging, but Thriva are bucking a trend to make pharmaceuticals cool. Inside their very pleasing test kit, the packaging had a unique pull mechanism that allowed the box to stretch out. The final component included a card with a hole in it where you could place your fingers inside to do a finger selfie. Not only did it have bags of personality but it included a call to action to tag them on Facebook, an easy mechanism to further spread the brand message.

WHO GIVES A CRAP

Who Gives a Crap is an Australian eco-friendly toilet paper brand on a subscription basis. Last year they designed a special play edition of 48 rolls in a large box, where each roll was different colourful heads, torsos and feet that you could stack to create characters. The overall box was pre-cut to create a little theatre – a fantastic example of clever use of packaging.

THE BEST OF THE REST

Three of the most popular ways we have extended our brand is through business books or e-books that showcase our expertise, podcasts or social media. We just wanted to leave you with a few final 'brand to life' tips on the most popular channels.

Business books

- Online sales are one of the biggest drivers for book sales. With this in mind, you need to spend more time than you realize looking at your cover thumbnail. When your book is just a sticker on a big web page, can you read it? Does it stand out?
- Who has written a book or content in a competitive space? You don't want to inadvertently have the same brand colours as them on your book. Look online or visit your local independent bookshop and have a look at the top ten books in your space. Check their covers. How can you differentiate yourselves from them?
- When briefing your book designer, ensure you are sending your branding toolkit as created in Chapters 1 and 2 and maybe add a slide or two of books that you like.

- Remember that your book is likely to have a shelf life of three to five years, so you don't want an image that can date too quickly.

Podcasts

- Check any trademarks around your podcast name before publishing.
- Is the editorial voice of your podcast in line with your brand and newly created brand values?
- Are you being inclusive with your guest list?
- Does the music fit your brand personality?
- How are you maximizing the shareability? Create an audiogram – these are smaller audio clips that can include a graphic sound bar to demonstrate there is dialogue or include subtitles of the content (try headliner.app or wavve.co.).

Social media avatars

We talked about bringing branding to life in your social media in Chapter 3, but just wanted to quickly look at creative ways to newsjack your avatar.

Could you ever temporarily change your social media avatar to react to the news agenda?

- In response to the COVID-19 pandemic of 2020, we saw socially distanced logos, like McDonald's separating their arches or Mercedes separating out their rings. This filtered down into more regional brands such as London magazine *Time Out* temporarily rebranding to *Time In*; or Sound Touch Change, where sound therapist Amanda

Jane crossed out the word 'touch' in her logo, to show that she was not offering massage and physical therapies during the height of the pandemic, but focusing on online sound therapy.

- Seasonal changes might also be an opportunity. For example, Simply Noir, the curated marketplace for black-owned business, temporarily changed their logo over the seasonal period by having a wreath around their thumbnail. It gave the feeling of a virtual Christmas shop.

CHAPTER SUMMARY

In this chapter, we've tried to dispel the myth that you need a huge budget to be creative and make a noise. We've highlighted some small businesses that we think have brought branding to life really well, with the aim of sparking some creativity for you and your business.

Like with everything, the more you practise, the easier it becomes. Maybe just start by playing around with some social or video content. If it doesn't work, and there is no traction, you've not lost anything – but it gives you an opportunity to start dipping your toe in the creative pool. With everything, it is important to keep flexing that creativity. Keep it topped up by consciously making an effort to look at the branding around you and save/collect things that inspire you.

CHAPTER 5

HOW TO BRIEF YOUR BRAND

At quite a few points over the last four chapters we've referenced getting external help with your brand, or various aspects of it, so we wanted to delve into when and how you should do this.

WHEN AND HOW TO WORK WITH EXTERNAL BRAND SUPPORT

Here are the most common frequently asked questions that you might want to think about before hiring someone to help with your brand.

WHEN SHOULD I HIRE A BRANDING AGENCY?

The answer is that it really depends. There's no point bankrupting yourself to create a brand before you have even started out; but, on the other hand, we know that trying to make a strong start with a poor brand makes life harder. The most obvious answer for when you should invest in your brand is when you have the money to invest! If funding is tight, we have seen some businesses use Kickstarter, or similar crowdfunding platforms, to build their brand.

Reminder: You can just have a working brand and brand name to get you started. Don't let fear of being brandless stop you from building your business. But do make sure you do a competitor check and make sure you are not infringing anyone else's trademark and copyright.

With the rise in small businesses and affordable design services, you don't have to work with a traditional branding agency to compile your whole brand. Instead, you might want to work with individuals on a one-to-one consulting basis to help you tweak the elements you have created from the activities and advice in this book.

For some of you, designing your own assets that represent your brand on Keynote or Canva is going to be super simple and clear and you might not need the visual branding help, but might need to work with someone on the brand positioning, values and mission. We've even introduced a branding-hour advice service where many small business owners present their visual brand to us and we can recommend tweaks to the colour palette, graphics, etc. to just help tighten things up.

Others of you will have zero problems in doing your mission, vision, purpose and audience work, but need some assistance in creating the visual work.

So, first, consider where your gaps are using this book and look at individuals that can assist in this space.

If you are looking at a more 'do it for you' approach – as in, you need to totally pass over the work to an expert – then this would lean more to picking a branding agency to work with. Traditional large branding agencies are used to budgets that run into tens of thousands per month and have the large offices and designer furniture and artwork to go with it! So I would look to pick a boutique branding agency that has lower overheads and therefore lower rates.

WHAT SHOULD I KNOW BEFORE REACHING FOR HELP?

Being super open to doing some of the brand strategy legwork before you move onto the visual creative work is really important. With someone's help, you can create something that looks great, but if it doesn't speak to your target audience or do what you need it to then it's not going to help your business. An agency or freelancer is not going to know your brand like you do, so you have to know it really well in order to help them to help you.

We also recommend that you create a checklist of what exactly you need help with and ensure that the package offered covers what you need. This might include:

- competitor search and name development, registering a trademark;
- brand strategy;
- editorial guidelines;
- brand visual guidelines (e.g. colours, font, images);
- personal branding photography;
- website design;
- SEO.

HOW DO I FIND THE RIGHT DESIGNER? HOW DO I KNOW IF SOMEONE IS GOOD?

A good place to start is your senses: what are you hearing and seeing? Word of mouth is a fantastic resource. Who talks about the great design experience they have had recently, or who they like working with?

Another way to go about this is, when you do your competitive research and mood board, you will come across brands that you think are doing fantastically well with their branding. Try Googling them to know who did their designs – especially if their brand feel is similar to yours.

But it's not just about finding a good designer, it's about finding the *right* one. As much good feedback as a designer gets, they might not be the right choice for *you*. The design process is a collaborative process; a unique bond must happen between you and the designer, like an intense friendship for just a few months. Not all great brand designers will be perfect for you. When you find someone promising, make sure to review their work, style and process, and have an in-depth interview with them before you commit.

We have found that using a creative platform like The Dots, a career network like LinkedIn or a closed business Facebook group can be a great source to ask people for their recommendations. Try posting something like this: 'I'm looking to work with a graphic designer for a project on XXX. Does anyone in my network know someone they have worked with that they can personally recommend?'

Personal recommendations are better than an industry's recommendation anyway, because the recommender will have had direct experience working with them. We can shout out hundreds of people whose creative work is excellent, but realistically, we have zero idea what it would be like to work for or with them. And when it comes to picking a freelance partner, it needs to be someone that you have a good feeling about and that you enjoy working with.

Final note: A good designer will be able to adapt their visual skills for your concept or audience, so don't worry about finding an agency or freelancer who has only worked with brands in your industry.

WHAT IS THE BEST WAY TO WORK WITH A DESIGNER OR CREATIVE?

For those of you who have already worked with creatives, this question might bring you some stressful memories. Trust me, I understand – I live and work with Hadrien! Many people in creative roles are speaking a different language to those of us in less creative industries: they come from a place of emotion and storytelling, and they live and breathe in a gigantic visual world where details and aesthetic balance have the most importance. And if that was not enough, the most crucial part of creating a good design is to fully immerse themselves in the brand they're working with, to connect to the deep emotion and values that run at its core – which means it can take a bit of time to adjust and fully connect.

Here are a few tips to get the most out of your working relationship with creatives:

- Communication and honesty are key.
- Don't be scared of oversharing.
- Be as precise as you can – provide examples and a mood board wherever possible. The more collaborative you can be right from the start, the easier it will be for the designer to gain an understanding of your vision.
- It might not be perfect at the first review, but that is ok.
- Judge the *work* not the *skills* – an important point for life in general actually!

- Give clear feedback – again, be as specific as you can about what is and what's not working and why.
- Be open to change or different points of view.

IS IT EXPENSIVE?

I'd encourage you to think about branding you *like* as opposed to branding you can *afford*. I say this because a senior designer with a lot of experience is obviously going to charge more, but they're not necessarily going to be the right fit for you anyway. If you don't like the senior designer's style, but love the portfolio of a junior, you may be better off with the junior, even if you have the biggest budget in the world.

The cost of a branding start-up package can vary hugely – from £2,000 to £70,000,[26] depending on the size of your brand, how many decision makers are involved, how long the project will take, what parts of the business will need a rebrand and so on. In the UK, creative recruiters Major Players[27] publish an annual salary survey report that shows you industry average day rates for freelancers. I find that this is a good starting point for gauging what you should be paying based on how many days' work they need for strategy and then visual design.

We can't stress enough that creating a strong brand is an investment. When you divide the cost up by how many days you intend to be in business, we are looking at just pence to look good.

---

[26] https://huglondon.com/insights/startup-branding-how-much-does-it-cost.
[27] www.majorplayers.co.uk/salary-survey-2021/.

Let's say you work with a specialist to do brand strategy work, create your brand for you and get a UK trademark and it costs £5,000. Over five years that works out at £2.73 a day – that's less than the price of a daily cup of coffee in London.[28]

DO I NEED TO GO TO DIFFERENT PEOPLE FOR WEBSITE, LOGO, BOOK COVER DESIGN, SOCIAL MEDIA BANNERS, ETC.?

Again, this comes down to budget. If you go to a boutique branding agency, for example, they will be able to offer all of these services and in some instances you might just want to use a freelancer to create one aspect of it. Where possible, it's always best practice to use the same person to cover everything, but this is why creating a list of the brand elements you need is useful – many freelancers or boutique agencies will have preferred partners or suppliers that they have worked well with and can recommend.

HOW DO I QUANTIFY SPENDING ON MY BRAND?

Big business currently leads the way in branding effective-ness; they can use expensive tools to measure branding awareness, share of market and have a really close eye on the numbers. They invest heavily on brand visibility – think about big companies sponsoring large sporting events just to have exposure to a wider audience.

---

[28] www.globalprice.info/en/?p=britan/prices-in-london-on-food.

For small businesses it's easier to measure something like a Facebook ad – you can instantly see if this is working for you by tracking the clicks, sales and page views. But when it comes to branding, brand building and PR, by its very nature it is not as quantifiable. That doesn't mean it's completely unmeasurable, though. Here are a few ways to track the effectiveness of your branding:

- *Surveys*. Learn from big brands and apply some of their techniques. Benchmark with your customers how memorable you are before the exercise (e.g. if they are clear about your values, your purpose, etc.). On a really basic level, just ask them what they like or remember about your business. Repeat the same exercise after the rebrand to gauge the change. You can also ask people how they heard about you or ask a random selection of people if they are familiar with your brand. Tools such as Typeform, Surveymonkey. com or Mentimetre can be good for this.
- *Traffic increase*. The idea of defining your brand and doing the strategy work in Chapter 1 is so that your visual and everything you do after this is memorable. With memorability comes connection, emotional attachment, growth and sales. Keep a monthly track of your audience size, website visits, newsletter growth and watch the difference before and after your rebrand. It's easy to be memorable when you have a consistent message. Website traffic, for example, and who has searched for you, is really easy to track by using Google Analytics.
- *Search volume*. This leads us nicely to Google Adwords Keyword Planner or Google Trends, where you can track if the volume of searches for your brand has increased.

- *Do you have slightly more budget?* If so, you might want to pay for or at least trial a social listening tool. It can give you an idea of the positive/negative things being said, the number of mentions and the reach of these (which could even then inform who you may want to collaborate with more/who is most effective for your brand). It can also do competitive analysis to see your share of voice against your competitors.

WHO ARE THE DIFFERENT BRANDING PEOPLE I MIGHT WORK WITH?

When it comes to working with a branding freelancer, it can be hard to know who to work with and at what point. There is also a lot of crossover between many of the roles in branding. We invited a few people from different roles within brand land to explain a bit about what it is they do and kickstarted with our own.

A creative director: Hadrien Châtelet

Just to add a little more confusion, the job title 'creative director' is used in TV, film, photography, advertising, music, as well as branding. But generally, for the work we are talking about, you need a creative director who works in design, branding or brand strategy. I've worked on everything from global corporate rebrands in multiple international markets, which includes heavy strategy and legal research on owning the name and brand, right down to a one-hour visual advice session on best practice for social media channels. Ultimately, what I love the most is taking the big agency strategic way of working and applying it visually by creating the assets and a toolkit for small businesses and start-ups, so that they can then use them easily themselves across all of their customer touchpoints and that it creates emotions, meaning and engaged loyal fans that return to that business. For me, the creative direction is the amalgamation of that strategy (direction) aligned with developing the visuals (creative).

A brand strategist: Amanda Appiagyei

As a brand strategist we work together to hone the foundational elements of your brand, the underwater part of the proverbial branding iceberg, which creates a solid brand strategy before the visual identity comes into play. This ensures you know exactly who your audience is, what they need from you and how you should communicate your offer or product to them. It includes things like your mission, your brand values, your tone of voice and brand personality, all of which help your audience to connect to your brand and make a decision to purchase. Your visual branding is the tip of the iceberg, the visual cue that your audience is in the right place. Together they create a strong, long-lasting brand.

A graphic designer: Sarah Boris

As well as a graphic designer, I am also an artist, lecturer and creative director. My project commissions include everything from visual identities, print and web design, exhibition graphics to signage. My work mainly involves bringing content to life in a creative way. The outcome can be a logo, magazine design or even a large poster campaign. A key element to working with a graphic designer is communication.

Another is transparency: talking the clients through steps such as the briefing, ideas, contract, payments, associated costs and the production process. The best way a small business owner should work with a graphic designer is with trust – I can't stress this enough. The more you trust the designer you work with, the better the results. I have found that whenever there is a lack of trust it bleeds into the design work and the design becomes a mishmash of compromises and is less strong. The chances are that once you have gone through the process of selecting a graphic designer, you will have chosen them because you like their work. My best designs have always been when the client has trusted me and the work has been uncompromised.

An illustrator: Lisa Tegtmeier

I'm a freelance illustrator and I work on illustrative commissions from international clients. I usually work on commercial or editorial projects, such as illustrating online and print articles or creating digital illustrations for websites, social media and advertising campaigns. There is definitely more freedom for me as an artist in illustration than graphic design. I see illustration as something in-between a service and art as I always put so much of myself and my point of view into my work. I usually get directly contacted by the brand or the businesses and they already come to me with a certain idea for a collaboration in mind. I always love to hear their thoughts and ideas about how they envision incorporating illustration into their project – it's super exciting. There are so many possibilities where and how illustrations can be included.

Art marketplace founder: Swakara Atwell-Bennett

I'm the founder and CEO of BetterShared, a contemporary African art marketplace. We help emerging artists sell their work. I also teach visual artists, illustrators and photographers how to market and monetize their work. The best way for a small business to work with an artist is to have an idea of what format, concept, style and budget they have. If you are not creatively minded, working with an agent can help you find an artist that could bring some new ideas to the table that perhaps you hadn't considered. A good brand is based on storytelling and this is the joy you get when you bring an artist into a brand, you get an added layer of thinking.

An artist: Amrit Singh

As a small business, creating a strong brand and presence is one of the key components in building a foundation that will allow you to flourish. One of the best ways to help you achieve this, is by working with designers and artists. The key differences between working with an artist and a designer is the process of developing the work, traditional and digital mediums and the social media influence you can potentially leverage. Knowing when to delegate and ask for help growing your businesses is really important. This is why I recommend considering commissioning or collaborating with an artist because they can help you with vital asset creation for your brand and website, understand overall colour theory and cross-collaboration and help elevate your brand to new audiences. However, if you decide to work with an artist, it's really important to work with their creativity, understand their strengths, have a clear brief and pay them the industry standard rate at a minimum.

Art director and typographer: Benoit Ollive

I am an art director and graphic designer who specializes in digital typography and lettering – both handmade and digital.

The designer side of my role is to find or create the best-suited fonts for the project to communicate the right aesthetic. I then develop all the necessary graphic elements in the form of a guideline presentation, specifying the use of those fonts, their colour, size and application to layouts for future use.

The art direction side of my role is to help develop a narrative around those elements, to communicate a story the audience can relate to and bring the brand to life with a rationale.

Typography is the simplest and most relatable, yet most complex piece of design, which is at the heart of everything. For a small business owner, owning a unique typography or logotype is a great way to stand out. You then own a piece of intellectual property for your business and a solid base to expand.

A copywriter: Matt Blake

I'm a journalist, copywriter and storytelling consultant. When it comes to working with small businesses, my job is to either polish or edit existing copy or to create brand messaging, editorial guidelines, blog posts, newsletter copy and sponsored editorial articles for magazines and newspapers (also called branded content). It's so easy for small business owners to overwrite content, because they're so close to the brand and sometimes struggle to separate what's important and what's not. So it's my job to try to smooth that out, bring clarity to their content and bring the business to life through words.

WHAT DO I PUT IN A BRIEF?

Some of the biggest challenges we see regarding briefs come from not enough depth and clarity. The best way to brief an external designer or creative is to show a clear understanding of your audience, what you would like to achieve and how. Who is this going to reach? What impact does it need to have? How do we need to achieve this? This last point is important: technically speaking, we often see people request branding assets without knowing the specifications they need. What size does it need to be, for example? Developing something for a 4 x 6 poster sheet is quite different to designing a thumbnail on a website.

Put as much detail as you can in your brief. Answer all the questions you can: who, what, why, when and how? An idea of timeline and budget can be really helpful and also often totally transform the brief. Finally, provide everything alongside the brief that the designer might need. Creating a folder of all assets is really handy; include any fonts they should be using, images, colours – everything they might need to work with. We can't stress enough how helpful, even at a basic level, preparing a mood board can be – and luckily, you should have loads of practice at that by now!

Here is a very basic checklist for determining whether your brief is ready to send out:

- Do you have a mood board?
- Have you got the copy ready?
- Do you know who your target audience is?
- What is your deadline?
- Do you know the number of pages required for a brochure, website or any other document? Changing the brief later on will throw off your budget and timelines.

Final note: Make sure there is a clear contract in place and that responsibility for problems or delays is shared between both sides. When it comes to creating a brand, delays in copy, client approval, revision of ideas, etc. can have a long-term impact on the original timeline – so make sure you have factored in contingency time.

HOW DO I WORK WITH A PRINTER?

My most saved post on Instagram was nothing to do with PR or branding, but about our printer – it turns out that sometimes what you think is the most interesting intel is different to what your audience wants to hear... but that is a whole other chapter! We have spent *weeks* researching printers. And just like everything else, cost is not always the most important factor – it is about quality and service. For us, that was Steve at Darwin Press.

When it comes to working with a printer, Steve is best placed to tell you about that – so we invited him to share some of his advice with us.

What are the common mistakes people make when briefing a printer?

Probably the most consistent mistake we come across involves briefing the printer too late or not briefing the printer at all until the project is finally signed off and ready to print. We would always advise people to talk to us as early as possible in the design process, preferably prior to presenting the visual work and concepts to the end client. This is most relevant in brochure work where the quantity will very much dictate the production method. We've had numerous occasions whereby a brochure has been designed to include spot Pantone colours and at a size that's not compatible to being printed digitally, when this would be by far the most cost-effective production method based on the quantity required.

Your printer will be best placed to offer help and advice on the most suitable production method(s), any issues with the proposed size or material choices, etc. Some of the best and often most cost-effective pieces of print we have produced are when we started collaborating at an early stage, thus avoiding a myriad of potential problems and pitfalls.

What are the things a novice should think about when briefing a printer?

The main point here is not to be afraid of asking too many questions! I'd recommend sending over a basic brief covering the main points and aspirations, but try not to include any technical aspects you don't fully understand. Give an overall explanation of what you are trying to achieve and ask your printer for their input, help and advice. For example, can they show you samples of any proposed finishes or offer alternatives that may work better or be more cost-effective? Wherever possible, request a dummy at the earliest opportunity. Most printers will offer these free of charge or for a small fee and it can save a lot of time, money and disappointment in the long run. It's in the printer's best interest to make sure your job exceeds all expectations and it's often at the briefing stage that this can be achieved.

Any key hints/tips? (I'm thinking about our classic mistake of printing all boxes first without cutting out our own mock-up before we pressed go, or people rushing and not allowing enough time...)

- It's always a good idea to see the final printed piece mocked up, if at all possible. If time doesn't allow for a physical mock-up, then ask the printer to send some images, preferably before going to print.
- If a project is time-sensitive, give your printer plenty of prior notice of its pending arrival. This will allow them to get stock ordered and book the job into their production schedule.
- Make sure your printer has all of the information needed when placing the order, particularly any specific delivery and/or packing instructions. This is often overlooked and can frustratingly lead to a delay in delivery at the final hurdle!

What is the most unusual thing you have ever made for a small business in terms of branding (if you can say)?
We've branded pretty much everything, from remote-controlled cars to cricket bats. Probably the most challenging and exciting is the work carried out for *The Apprentice*, producing everything from branded stickers and food packaging to display graphics for the individual teams. We do actually have to produce this overnight for delivery to the house the following morning!

What are the most common things you are asked to print for branding/small businesses?
The most common branded items are notepads/books, laptop stickers, pens/pencils and tote bags.

Any future print trends/examples that small businesses can learn from?
Digital print has enabled far more flexibility in terms of personalization and allows companies to more easily target individuals or a specific sector. Rather than printing 1,000 generic brochures, we're now far more likely to print smaller quantities with the content aimed at smaller, specific groups.

Likewise, recipients are much more likely to spend time reading and understanding your correspondence if it has their name on it. As soon as your customer spots their name on a leaflet or postcard, they'll be intrigued by its contents, giving direct mail campaigns a far better chance of success in boosting enquiries and orders.

This is a great way for small businesses to use print far more cost-effectively in their marketing campaigns.

Printer's brief

We also spoke to Steve about the correct information you need to include in a brief for the printer. Bearing in mind the fact that one size doesn't fit all, he has given us a basic template to share with you. You can see the full template in our downloadable playbook, but here are some top-line points to think about including in your printer's brief:

Printer's brief template	
Job title	
Quantity	
Finished size **Flat size**	
Orientation	*Portrait or landscape?*
Number **of pages** (including cover if applicable)	
Number of **printed colours**	*E.g. four colours (CMYK), five colours* *(CMYK + one-spot Pantone)*
Materials **(including** **weight)**	*E.g. 350 gsm silk*
Cover	
Text	
Binding **method**	*E.g. Saddle stitched* *PUR bound* *Section sewn* *Wire bound* *Other (please specify)*
Any special **finishes**	*E.g. laminations, spot UVs, foils, etc.*
Delivery date **and address**	

CHAPTER SUMMARY

In this chapter, we've aimed to show you some of the ways you can work with different branding individuals and given some hints and tips on briefing external parties. Working with a third party on your brand is a partnership; it requires give and take on both sides. If you are hiring an expert to consult on your brand, you should be willing to listen to their constructive critique of your current brand position. Remember, this is what they do for a job, and they want you to do well, so try not to take offence. But equally, if you feel your branding partner just doesn't get you and who you are, then sometimes it's better to find someone that you do have that connection with. If you happen to stumble across an individual or an agency that does great work for you: shout about them! This ticks your authority box in personal branding and helps you shine a spotlight on someone else. Sharing personal recommendations is great small business and branding karma all round.

CHAPTER 6

BRAND ON!

Congratulations! You have now reached the end of your branding toolkit journey. We set out to try and teach you the importance of branding, walk you through how to create your assets, think about how you can link your business and personal brand to maximize your reach and finished with some creative ways you could think about bringing your brand out into the wild. Last but not least, we have given some hints and tips from our own experience and that of others in our industry on how best to work with branding professionals.

Revising The Wern brand in January 2019, alongside hyping ourselves, was a catalyst that changed our business. We went from just being a service-based agency model to providing consulting services, being booked for guest lectures, hosting workshops, being approached by partners and ultimately attracting more of the customers we want to work with. It allowed us to pivot the work we do to fit around our two children, and it meant we could stop using a business model based on our time for money, which obviously gets capped because we only have a certain number of hours in a day.

Today, revisiting our brand strategy we identified that we have two audiences. Which is why we then split our business into two. TheWern.com is for startups and scale-ups where we do the consultancy for them and HypeYourself.com which is our freelance and small business audience looking for DIY support.

We are not saying that nailing your brand is going to be the solution to all your business problems, but we do know that industrywide we are seeing a brilliant and growing trend towards business with purpose. If you don't understand the meaning behind why you are doing what you are doing and who you want to serve, then you are missing a trick.

Small businesses are really well placed to take ownership of their brand, tell their story and share their values because they are not constricted by corporate red tape. They can also react quickly to the news agenda and make sure that their meaning is centre stage.

If we could leave you with one final note on your brand to take away, it's this: it is not about your logo, it's not even about what you look like. It is the *feeling* you give; it's how you make people feel after they have interacted with you. When you go out into the world after today, always ask yourself, when it comes to any work you do, people you partner with, the books you recommend, the influencers you work with – does this really fit my brand? Hell yes or hell no! You have an opportunity to grow your brand in every single activity that you do. Make sure it fits your bigger purpose.

Our mission is to help provide affordable, big-agency brand experience for small businesses, and we hope that this book has helped to do just that.

KEY TERMS

SOFTWARE

Adobe Acrobat Software from the Adobe family to edit and create pdf files as well as generate digital forms.

Adobe Illustrator Software from the Adobe family to design vector graphics, logos and layouts.

Adobe InDesign Software from the Adobe family to design and set up print layouts like brochures, books, magazines, etc.

Adobe Photoshop Software from the Adobe family to retouch, resize or recolour images.

Adobe XD Software from the Adobe family used as a vector graphics editor and prototyping tool, primarily for developing websites and applications.

Canva An online graphic design platform to create social media visuals, presentations and brochures from scratch or from templates.

Figma A vector graphics editor and prototyping tool primarily used for developing websites and applications.

Sketch A wireframe builder and vector graphics editor for developing websites and applications only on macOS.

FILES

AI Editable vector files generated by Adobe Illustrator.

CMYK (cyan, magenta, yellow, black) Colour values for print documents. You will need to convert your files to CMYK if you are working on a print document.

dpi (dots per inch) or resolution The density of pixels per inch in a pixelated image. For a digital artwork we normally set the artwork from 72 dpi to 150 dpi; for a print artwork we set at 300 dpi or above.

EPS (encapsulated postscript) Generic editable vector files used by all design software.

GIF (graphics interchange format) Similar characteristics as a PNG but is usually used for small animation, like you will find on an Instagram story.

JPEG (joint photographic expert group) Generic pixel files, non-editable.

MOV Larger video files generated by QuickTime File Format.

MP4 Small video files.

PDF (portable document format) Generic vector files used by all design software, usually used for print documents.

Pixels The millions of tiny squares that form an image. They can be red, green or blue, then put together generate an infinite range of colours. The quantity, size and colour combination of pixels varies and is measured in terms of the display resolution.

PNG (portable network graphics) Small graphic or simple image files, used mainly in a digital environment. They have the great bonus of being able to have a transparent background.

PSD (photoshop document) Editable pixel image files generated by Adobe Photoshop.

RGB (red, green, blue) Colour values for digital documents. You will need to convert your files to RGB if you are working on digital artwork.

Vector (or vector graphic/image) Artwork made of precisely defined shapes, like lines, rectangles, curves or points, with plain or gradient colours. They are created using back-end mathematical codes. They can be scaled up or down without losing their quality and are used for creating logos and graphics. There are generated using Adobe Illustrator, Corel Drawn and other vector software.

TYPOGRAPHY

align left, right, centre When all the lines of a text are aligned to the left, right or centred.

condensed Letters, numbers or glyphs of a condensed font have set widths that are narrower than in the standard typeface from the same family.

contrast The difference between the thicker part and the finer part of a letter, number or glyph.

extended Letters, numbers or glyphs of an extended font have set widths that are wider than in the standard typeface from the same family.

font family All the weights and variations of a particular font.

font weight The thickness of the letters, numbers or glyphs. For example, you can have extra light, light, regular, medium, bold, extra bold.

glyphs All the symbols used to communicate excluding letters and numbers (e.g. @ # , : ' } – & ...).

justify left, right, or centred When all the lines of a paragraph are aligned to the left, right or centred on the page and some extra space between the words is added by the software so that both edges of each line are aligned with both margins.

italic or slant When the typeface is leaning forwards.

kerning The space between each letter.

leading The height between each line.

typeface or font The design of letters, numbers and glyphs.

BRANDING AND DESIGN

art board The generic name given to an on-screen design surface. Often designers will show you their art board where they have designed all the logo variations for you to choose from.

avatar Another word for your audience – the representation of your perfect customer.

brand guidelines A printed or digital document that highlights all the elements and rules of your brand, from strategy, logo usage, colour values, imagery dos and don'ts and much more, depending on your brand needs.

brand world All the elements or touchpoints that your audience will experience (e.g. colours, fonts, images, sound, tone of voice, etc.).

logo A word or icon that a company or individual uses to be remembered and instantly recognized.

look and feel All the visual elements that create your brand world, excluding your logo.

mark or emblem The conceptual representation of the brand, usually used alongside the logo.

USEFUL RESOURCES

apstylebook.com AP Stylebook – style guidelines resource for journalists and publications.

behance.net A search tool for photos, videos, logos, illustrations and branding – very helpful for creating a mood board.

canva.com A great tool for helping to create marketing materials for your brand, including presentations, flyers, social media posts, etc. You can use the 'brand toolkit' function to upload your own toolkit or get inspiration from their own on-trend colour palettes.

color.adobe.com/create/color-accessibility If you have access to Adobe, you can check the new accessibility tools for colour selection.

colororacle.org A free colour-blind simulator check.

colourcontrast.cc A site for you to check your colour palette and make sure that the colour contrast is accessible.

colours.cafe Offers helpful suggestions if you are struggling to find your brand colour palette.

copy.ai A great resource if you need help crafting headlines, blog posts, copy material, etc.

creativemarket.com Provides a wide selection of unique fonts starting from very affordable costs for small business owners.

dyslexic.com/blog/quick-guide-making-content-accessible Long-form content with no spacing can make text really tricky for a dyslexic person to read. Check this great article for hints and hacks to make your copy more accessible.

fonts.google.com A free resource to find fonts.

forbes.com/diversity-equity-inclusion A selection of great articles to help you on your diversity, equity and inclusion journey.

myfonts.com Provides a wide selection of unique fonts starting from very affordable costs for small business owners.

namecheckr.com A tool that allows you to check which social media handles have already been taken.

wavve.co An audiogram app (turn your audio into video – great for podcasts).

RECOMMENDED READING

Pragya Agarwal, *Sway: Unravelling Unconscious Bias* (2020)

David Airey, *Identity Designed: The Definitive Guide to Visual Branding* (2019)

Drew de Soto, *Know Your Onions: Graphic Design* (2014)

David Hieatt, *Do Open: How a Simple Email Newsletter Can Transform Your Business (and It Can)* (2017)

Laura Kalbag, *Accessibility for Everyone* (2017)

Robert Klanten and Anna Sinofzik (eds), *Start Me Up! New Branding for Businesses* (2015)

Radim Malinic, *Book of Branding: A Guide to Creating Brand Identity for Start-Ups and Beyond* (2019)

Marty Neumeier, *The Brand Flip: Why Customers Now Run Companies and How to Profit from It* (2015)

Marty Neumeier, *Brand Gap: The Revised Edition* (2005)

Daniel Priestly, *Oversubscribed: How to Get People Lining Up to Do Business with You* (2015)

Simon Sinek, *Start With Why* (2009)

Shireen Smith, *Brand Tuned: The New Rules of Branding, Strategy and Intellectual Property* (2021)

Lucy Werner, *Hype Yourself: A No-Nonsense PR Toolkit for Small Businesses* (2020)

ACKNOWLEDGEMENTS

I don't think I can thank Alison and the team at Practical Inspiration Publishing enough for taking us on for the second time. I pinged her a proposal after a few too many rosés, a few days after getting engaged, and her full faith in our ability to do this really spurred us on.

All my followers on social media channels who constantly help me by fielding questions, responding to polls and inadvertently showing me all the time what is popular content or not by engaging with us – you have been the true inspiration for creating this book.

To everyone who contributed and who I always chased at the eleventh hour for amendments or copy approval, thank you for your endless patience. Thanks also to our extended team: Paula, who organizes my diary and forced me to get this over the line despite challenging circumstances; and our lovely Amy, whose creativity, joy and team support quite frankly make her more like part of the family.

www.ingramcontent.com/pod-product-compliance
Lightning Source LLC
Jackson TN
JSHW011948131224
75386JS00042B/1612